Ways to use this prayer guide

We always pray better together.
Over 150,000 believers from many hundreds of churches will be praying these prayers. So you won't be praying alone.

Find and share practical ideas.
Use the helpful resources at **waymakers.org**. Find practical ways to remind your church family to pray, such as bulletin inserts and powerpoint slides. Interact with others about what you like about the prayers at **Facebook.com/seekgodforthecity**.

The Spanish translation
Invite Spanish-speaking friends to pray with *Seek God for the City* in Spanish. It's called *Clama a Dios por la Ciudad 2015*. The 64-page booklet is available at the same low cost as the English version. Available December 2014.

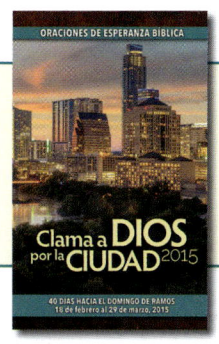

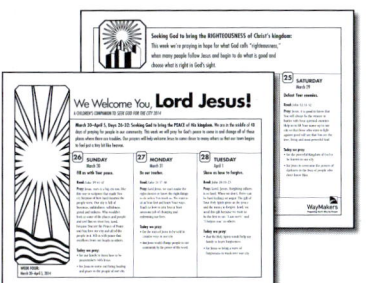

Pray with the kids: A children's version.
A free, downloadable kid's version is available in "pdf" format on our website. It's a great resource to engage kids in this prayer adventure! Find it at **waymakers.org**.

Pray as you go: Get the companion app.
Get *Seek God 2015* as an app on your tablet or smartphone. The app contains all of the same scriptures, prayers and helpful material. The app makes it even more flexible and accessible. Available December 2014. Check out a preview at **waymakers.org**. Tell your friends in other cities and countries about the app.

 iOS   Android

The beginnings of **Seek God for the City**

Why 40 days to Palm Sunday?

by Steve Hawthorne

I vividly remember the moment in the summer of 1994. I was in San Francisco, praying with my friend Mike Griffiths at the old mission in the heart of the city. As we prayed, an idea formed: To mobilize many to united, mission-focused prayer, we could organize a prayerwalk through the whole city. But suddenly the idea took full form: We would, with a team of 40 people, traverse the entire length of the colonial era highway in California known as *El Camino Real* ("The King's Highway"), more than 800 miles from San Diego to San Francisco.

We knew that the old imperial highway known as *El Camino Real* had been formed in the late 18th century to claim California for a European crown. Since gold would not be discovered until 1849, Franciscan missionaries were given freedom to build a chain of mission stations designed to evangelize native Indian tribes. The road quickly became the backbone of California's history. By prayerwalking this crucial highway, labeled long ago with a prophetic significance to be "The King's Highway," we hoped to dramatize both God's coming in visitation and His sending in mission.

PAGE 2

A prophetic and practical prayer venture 20 years ago
The California Prayerwalk

We brought together a team of 40 people that was multi-denominational, multi-racial and multi-generational (a grandmother, her daughter and her three grand-daughters). It was anything but a prayer stunt. Instead, it was a prophetic enactment as well as a practical demonstration of praying for every person throughout a community. The team prayed step-by-step along the entire highway, joined for brief segments by thousands of others along the way.

In keeping with the idea of welcoming Christ as king, we sensed God leading us to culminate on Palm Sunday (see pages 48-49 to know why). We had the idea that we would finish it in 40 days. So the dates were fixed: 40 days to Palm Sunday, March 1 through April 9, 1995.

To support this prayer expedition, we formed a new mission structure, calling it "WayMakers." The purpose of WayMakers has always been to mobilize God's people to pray and labor for the global glory of Christ and the blessing of the nations.

To help unite prayer during the 40 days in 1995, we put together a 40-day prayer guide with biblical ideas for prayer for each day. Hundreds of people united their prayers with this tool. Many asked if we could publish something like it again. So the next year we published a freshly-written 40-day prayer guide called, *Seek God for the City '96*. Thousands were used right away with increasing interest almost every year. We have published more than two million copies since then. You hold in your hand the 20th edition of *Seek God for the City*.

WEEK 1   FEBRUARY 18 - FEBRUARY 28

PRAYING TOWARD HOPE
REVIVAL of GOD'S PEOPLE

This "week" (actually 11 days, beginning on Ash Wednesday, February 18) we will pray that God will revive His people as He has done before in history, and as He has promised in scripture. For anyone to pray with authentic expectation that God will bring this kind of profound change amidst His people calls for bold, biblically-informed hope. Take courage; many thousands of people will be reading these scriptures and praying these prayers with open-hearted sincerity. Let's pray together with expectancy through the next 40 days.

THE AMERICAS AND THE CARIBBEAN

During the 40 days, we will be praying for the continental areas of the earth in reverse sequence of Acts 1:8. Thus, we begin at one of the areas of the earth farthest from Jerusalem. We will start by praying for the continents of South and North America and the Caribbean.

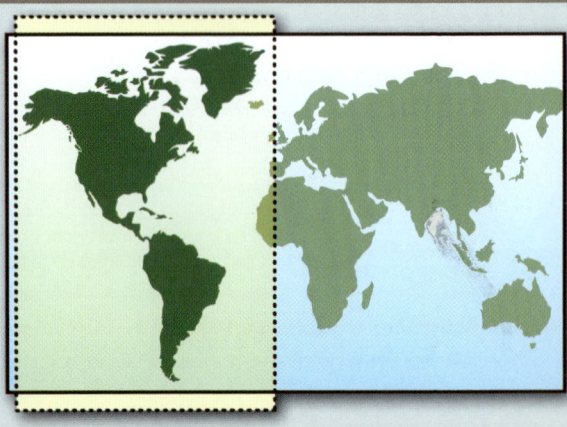

Seek God...
to bring lasting revival

DAY 1
WEDNESDAY
FEBRUARY 18

*Will You not revive us again, that Your people may rejoice in You? Show us Your unfailing love, O LORD...
I will listen to what God the LORD will say;
He promises peace to His people, His saints
– but let them not return to folly.
Surely His salvation is near those who fear Him,
that His glory may dwell in our land.* — Psalm 85:6-9

Once again we seek to be renewed. It is a prayer we have prayed before: Revive us again! Dare we ask that You would revive Your people once and for all? Revivals in earlier generations have come and gone, blazing intensely and then sputtering out. Can Your unfailing love bring an unceasing revival? We know that our love for You fades, but Your love is never-failing. Show us what Your enduring love can do. Speak in life-giving power and lift our fluttering hopes. Bring Your promised peace upon us. Save us in ways that surprise us. Envelop entire cities with resurrection life so that Your glory shines throughout our land.

· ·

*Go on before the Lord to prepare His ways,
to give to His people the knowledge of salvation
by the forgiveness of their sins, because of the
tender mercy of our God, with which the Sunrise
from on high shall visit us.* — Luke 1:76-78 (NASB)

In times past You have surprised Your people by bringing Your presence upon them with a love that they didn't expect. It was as if the brilliant light of the sun had suddenly descended from the sky, exposing forgotten and hidden sins to the forgiving love of God. Get us ready to be amazed by the intensity and newness of Your mercy. Visit us with Your reviving love. *Pray:*

- For God to expose sin in ways that bring hope that we will be set free from its power.
- For Christians to be awakened to expect God to visit entire communities with life-giving mercy.

SEEK GOD ON BEHALF OF
YOUTH

Then our sons in their youth will be like well-nurtured plants, and our daughters will be like pillars carved to adorn a palace. ...Blessed are the people whose God is the LORD.
— Psalm 144:12, 15

For teens to radically and completely commit their lives to Christ; to make wise choices; for older mentors; for authentic friendships with their peers who are following Jesus; for open trust and communication with parents; for God's intentions for their generation to come forth in fullest measure.

· ·

PRAYERWALK: Pray with your eyes open for people in their teens. Envision them following Christ five, ten or more years from now.

SEEK GOD
ON BEHALF OF

THE AMERICAS
AND THE CARIBBEAN

Anguilla, Antigua and Barbuda, Argentina, Aruba, Bahamas

DAY 2

THURSDAY
FEBRUARY 19

Seek God...
for humility to replace our pride and complacency

SEEK GOD ON BEHALF OF
MARRIAGES

Marriage should be honored by all.
— Hebrews 13:4

Thank God for sturdy marriages that reflect His faithfulness and beauty. Pray especially for marriages which are strained to a breaking point or are failing, that God will bring both hope and help; that He will heal broken hearts and restore intimacy; for every marriage, that God will refresh and re-center homes in Christ.

PRAYERWALK: *Pray for the married couples living in your neighborhood.*

SEEK GOD ON BEHALF OF
THE AMERICAS AND THE CARIBBEAN

Barbados, Belize, Bermuda, Bolivia, Brazil

These people come near to Me
  with their mouth and honor Me with their lips,
  but their hearts are far from Me.
Their worship...is made up only of rules taught by men.
Therefore once more I will astound these people
  with wonder upon wonder.
The wisdom of the wise will perish;
the intelligence of the intelligent will vanish.
— Isaiah 29:13-14

We know what it is like to be impressed by our own religious performance. We can say all the correct words, yet leave our hearts far behind. We are so well-rehearsed in worship routines that they have become predictable and safe. We are among those who have approached You without heart or humility. Please break through our pride. Gather our wayward hearts. Surprise us with Your supremacy. Stun us with how dangerous You are. Ravish us with the brilliance of Your beauty so that the cloud of clever religious pride evaporates in the radiance of Your glory.

Come to Me...Take My yoke upon you and learn from Me, for I am gentle and humble in heart, and you will find rest for your souls. — Matthew 11:28-29

Not only have we kept ourselves busy, we have actually taken pride in how preoccupied we have become. But our ambitious self-sufficiency leaves us weary and distracted. We come to You now, just as You have summoned us to come–close enough to learn who You are. Show us Your heart and train us in Your humility. *Pray:*

- For God to intercept our runaway lives so that we can be trained in the ways of Christ's heart.
- For Christ's humility to replace deeply-rooted pride.

Seek God...
to break the power of sin

DAY 3

FRIDAY
FEBRUARY 20

*If You, O LORD, kept a record of sins...who could stand?
But with You there is forgiveness...
My soul waits for the Lord more than watchmen
wait for the morning...Put your hope in the LORD,
   for with the LORD is unfailing love
   and with Him is full redemption.
He Himself will redeem Israel from all their sins.*
— Psalm 130:3-8

You have wiped away our sins in Christ, so that there is no longer a record of our wrongdoing. We stand in grateful awe of Your mighty forgiving mercy. But we also stand in hope, yearning for even more. Not only have You pardoned our sins, but You continue to work in us, in order to free us from the dreadful power of sin. We focus our hearts to hope, watching confidently for Your work, as if we were waiting for daybreak. We cannot imagine that You will fail to fully redeem Your people. Cause us to live and to love like You!

* * *

*Jesus said to them,
"It is not the healthy who need a doctor, but the sick.
I have not come to call the righteous, but sinners."*
— Mark 2:17

You have called us away from spiritual sickness to live in Your righteous ways. You called us, not because we were better than any others, but because we were more sin-sick than most. We count ourselves among those whom You are still healing. Come again to our community, Great Physician, and make a house call in our city to free many from subtle, stubborn habits of sin. *Pray:*

- For people to be freed from devastating patterns of habitual sin.
- For the call of Christ to reach people who are eager to be freed from the power of sin.

SEEK GOD ON BEHALF OF
UNEMPLOYED PEOPLE

Everyone may eat and drink, and find satisfaction in all his toil — this is the gift of God.
— Ecclesiastes 3:13

That God will meet the needs of those without work in a way that they can clearly thank God for His provision; that they will soon find meaningful employment and glorify God for it; that God will open the way for righteous trade so that the entire city prospers in His provision.

PRAYERWALK: *Pray for those in your neighborhood who have recently lost their job or are struggling to find one.*

SEEK GOD ON BEHALF OF
THE AMERICAS AND THE CARIBBEAN

British Virgin Islands, Canada, Cayman Islands, Chile, Colombia

DAY 4

SATURDAY
FEBRUARY 21

Seek God...
to purify our hearts

SEEK GOD ON BEHALF OF
PASTORS

Be shepherds of God's flock that is under your care… Cast all your anxiety on Him because He cares for you.
— 1 Peter 5:2, 7

That pastors and church leaders will be filled with wisdom; that they will be honored by those they serve; that God will pour His Spirit upon them in power and humility, giving fresh intimacy with Jesus; for protection from the plots of the evil one against their families; that deep friendships with other pastors will grow.

PRAYERWALK: *Pray outside a church building for the pastor(s) who serve(s) that church.*

SEEK GOD ON BEHALF OF
THE AMERICAS AND THE CARIBBEAN

Costa Rica, Cuba, Dominica, Dominican Republic, Ecuador

*Create in me a clean heart, O God,
and renew a steadfast spirit within me…
Restore to me the joy of Your salvation
and sustain me with a willing spirit.*
— Psalm 51:10,12 (NASB)

We have blamed others for contaminating our community, but we find compromise and hidden sin in our own hearts. We long to be clean and free. Search us to find secret areas of sin. Purify us from the inside out. Grant us enduring spiritual power to serve You with integrity. We long for the joy of a single-minded devotion to You, our most Holy God.

A man with leprosy came to Him and begged Him on his knees, "If You are willing, You can make me clean." Filled with compassion, Jesus reached out His hand and touched the man. "I am willing," He said. "Be clean!"
— Mark 1:40-41

Lord Jesus, You are just as willing to cleanse us now from the pollution of sin as You were ready to heal people from leprosy long ago. Many of our community, Christians included, continue to struggle with sin. We pray for ourselves, as well as many others, to be clean and free from what defiles us from within. You are still filled with compassion. You are willing to touch us. You can make us clean. *Pray:*

- For God to give us, and others throughout our city, a desire to be free from sin.
- That Christ's compassion would be revealed to those who feel hopeless and alone in their shame.

Seek God...
to pour out fresh rivers of His Spirit

DAY 5

SUNDAY
FEBRUARY 22

For I will pour water on the thirsty land, and streams on the dry ground; I will pour out My Spirit on your offspring, and My blessing on your descendants. They will spring up like grass in a meadow, like poplar trees by flowing streams. – Isaiah 44:3-4

Pour out Your Spirit with slow, steady abundance, so that many streams begin to flow through desolate places. Cause many who are lifeless and dry to be awakened by the work of Your Spirit. Divert a gentle river from heaven upon our entire city. Inundate us with Your love. Soak us with steady streams so that what lies dormant now will bloom in a soon-coming day of blessing. Bring the outpouring of Your life on our children. Keep the river running through their lives so that they will grow as strong and tall as trees.

* * *

Jesus stood and said in a loud voice: "If anyone is thirsty, let him come to Me and drink. Whoever believes in Me, as the Scripture has said, streams of living water will flow from within him." – John 7:37-38

Take Your stand again in our city. Raise Your voice so that every person can hear Your word. You speak in ways that surpass all human understanding. Call us to come. Call us to slake our thirst in You. Let many come to You and cause them to drink deeply and live. Transform all who believe to become streams, and then rivers of life. You are the source, but let us be the course through which You send Your Spirit's life to many more. *Pray:*

- For believers to be life-giving streams of God's Spirit.
- For great spiritual thirst throughout our city, nation and world.
- For many to hear the voice of Jesus calling them to come and drink.

SEEK GOD ON BEHALF OF
ORPHANS

You have heard the desire of the humble. You will strengthen their heart. You will incline Your ear to vindicate the orphan and the oppressed.
– Psalm 10:17-18 (NASB)

Pray for children who have lost their parents, or who are now in foster care away from their birth parents; for safe, loving, permanent homes with godly adoptive or foster parents; for healing from any effects of physical, emotional or sexual abuse; for siblings to be adopted together; for thousands of young people who have already "aged out" of adoptive services, that they will find wise mentors and a secure place in the family of God.

PRAYERWALK: *In many neighborhoods God is calling people to become foster or adoptive parents. Pray that they act in His grace, love and wisdom.*

SEEK GOD
ON BEHALF OF

THE AMERICAS AND THE CARIBBEAN

El Salvador, Falkland Islands, French Guiana, Greenland

DAY 6

MONDAY
FEBRUARY 23

Seek God...
to stir us to persistent, united prayer

SEEK GOD ON BEHALF OF
SICK PEOPLE

He saw a large crowd, and felt compassion for them and healed their sick.
— Matthew 14:14 (NASB)

That God will touch those who are sick in your community with healing and comfort; that they will grow in grace as God walks with them throughout their ordeal; that God will provide for their financial needs; for their caregivers and families; that many will renew their trust in Christ and follow Him boldly, even in affliction.

PRAYERWALK: *Consider those who may be struggling with chronic illness or pain in your neighborhood. Pray for their healing.*

SEEK GOD ON BEHALF OF
THE AMERICAS AND THE CARIBBEAN

Grenada, Guadeloupe, Guatemala, Guyana, Haiti

I have posted watchmen on your walls, O Jerusalem. They will never be silent day or night.
You who call on the LORD, give yourselves no rest, and give Him no rest till He establishes Jerusalem and makes her the praise of the earth.
— Isaiah 62:6-7

What You have promised to do in the cities and peoples of the earth is vast and precious. We refuse to believe that You are finished with what You intend to do in our community. Do something so remarkable that Your name will be spoken of with praise in faraway places for what You have done in our midst. Lift our failing hopes so that we pray beyond our personal needs. Grant us stamina to stick to our post, asking, watching and thanking You. Give us prayers, large and small, that call forth Your coming days of praise.

...that at all times they ought to pray and not to lose heart. — Luke 18:1 (NASB)

We have condemned ourselves for prayerlessness, often blaming our full and busy lives. But we have not been overwhelmed by our schedules as much as we have lost heart that You will indeed fulfill what You have promised. Call us anew to a life of praying with steady determination. Our own resolve is not enough. Energize us with Your unwavering zeal. Let us know how pleased You are with our feeble attempts to pray with persistence. Train us to pray in patient pursuit of Your promises. *Pray:*

- For Christ to encourage our hearts to pray with renewed hope and persistence.
- For God to invigorate new seasons of prayer in our families, churches and cities.

Seek God...
to reveal His glory amidst His people

DAY 7

TUESDAY
FEBRUARY 24

Arise, shine; for your light has come,
*   and the glory of the LORD has risen upon you.*
For behold, darkness will cover the earth
*   and deep darkness the peoples;*
but the LORD will rise upon you and His glory
*   will appear upon you.*
Nations will come to your light,
*   and kings to the brightness of your rising.*
                              – Isaiah 60:1-3 (NASB)

The flickering flames of our own goodness cannot dispel the shadow of spiritual darkness that engulfs our community. Bring on Your reviving, exposing light, like the rising of the sun. Prepare us as worthy reflectors of Your beauty. Rise like a slow-coming dawn upon us, so that a great reflected glory will overwhelm the murky dullness of our city. Draw men, women and children to Your brightness.

* * *

I have given them the glory that You gave Me,
that they may be one as We are one.   – John 17:22

If this statement was not in the Bible, we would have thought it blasphemy to touch, much less to wear, the glory of Jesus. But Your purpose is clear: that we would carry the beauty, the power, the brilliance and the substance of who You really are. Confirm and mature this awesome gift of imparted glory. May the shining uniqueness of Your character be displayed in our city by those who name You as Lord. Unite Your churches as one so that together we become a spectacle of many people following One Magnificent Person. *Pray:*

- For Christ's justice, mercy and holiness to be seen in His people.
- That different churches would support and honor each other in displays of tangible unity.
- For Christians to reflect the integrity and character of Jesus in the marketplace.

SEEK GOD ON BEHALF OF
THE MILITARY

A centurion came to Him, asking for help….When Jesus heard this, He was astonished and said…"I tell you the truth, I have not found anyone in Israel with such great faith."
                              – Matthew 8:5-10

For the gospel to spread through the special relationships of military life; for courage and protection in the danger of battle; for wisdom and the fear of the Lord when military personnel are called upon to do the work of governing and enforcing law; for grace upon chaplains and other spiritual leaders; that God will fortify families stretched by numerous moves and separations.

PRAYERWALK: *Pray near a military base or establishment.*

SEEK GOD ON BEHALF OF
THE AMERICAS AND THE CARIBBEAN

Honduras, Jamaica, Martinique, Mexico, Montserrat

DAY 8

WEDNESDAY
FEBRUARY 25

Seek God...
to renew our passion to worship

SEEK GOD ON BEHALF OF
ARTS AND ENTERTAINMENT

He has filled him with the Spirit of God, with skill, ability and knowledge in all kinds of crafts...to engage in all kinds of artistic craftsmanship.
— Exodus 35:31-33

That God will inspire artists and entertainers with creativity and wisdom that reflect God's beauty; that they will seek God and come to follow Christ with courage; that their work will bring strength, goodness and hope to our communities.

PRAYERWALK: *Visit an art museum, a theater, or a place of entertainment for the purpose of praying for the artists or those working in support capacities.*

SEEK GOD
ON BEHALF OF

THE AMERICAS AND THE CARIBBEAN

Netherlands Antilles, Nicaragua, Panama, Paraguay, Peru

But may all who seek You rejoice and be glad in You; may those who love Your salvation always say, "Let God be exalted!" — Psalm 70:4

We love Your salvation. You have saved our souls from destruction. You are saving our families from falling apart. You are lifting our minds from depression and despair. You are preserving us for a day of even greater salvation. We love the relentless way that You save us. You deserve far more than an occasional "Thank You" from a few. Fill our city with lasting gratitude toward You. We want You to be greatly known, undeniably revealed, vastly followed and lavishly honored. And so with one voice we cry, "Let God be exalted in our lives! May Jesus Christ be exalted as the Savior of the world!"

At that time Jesus, full of joy through the Holy Spirit, said, "I praise You, Father, Lord of heaven and earth..." — Luke 10:21

Lord Jesus, You worshiped the Father with passionate gladness. We want to worship with the same joy that gave You such great delight. Open our eyes to see what pleases the Father. May the Holy Spirit fill us in the same way that He filled You, so that we can be a people overflowing with joyful praise to the Father. *Pray:*

- For joy to be renewed in believers who struggle with depression.
- That God would be openly praised by His people.
- For Christians to worship with joy, in the power of the Holy Spirit.

Seek God...
to renew our hearts to obey Him

DAY 9

THURSDAY
FEBRUARY 26

I will give you a new heart and put a new spirit in you;
I will remove from you your heart of stone
and give you a heart of flesh.
And I will put My Spirit in you and move you
to follow My decrees and be careful to keep My laws.
— Ezekiel 36:26-27

Hear us on behalf of people who have become discouraged and have drifted away from You. Some have been enticed by the world, while others feel that they have been wounded by the church. However they may have strayed from You, we ask that they will live again. We, too, have known the misery of a stony heart. With genuine humility we pray for them, that You would fulfill Your ancient promise to change hearts of stone. Cause Your Spirit to come upon us all so that we become eager to obey You as never before.

"Love the Lord your God with all your heart
and with all your soul and with all your mind
and with all your strength." The second is this:
"Love your neighbor as yourself." There is no
commandment greater than these. — Mark 12:30-31

Imprint this command on our hearts as a promise, as a destiny, as a certain hope. We shall love God! We shall love our neighbors! But we are dismayed to find that conflicting loyalties divide the affections of our hearts. Our souls are tainted with things You hate. Our minds are compromised with falsehoods. Our strength is wasted on lesser things. Even though we have failed to love as You desire, we ask that You would enable and empower us to love as never before. *Pray:*

- For many to be encouraged by the genuine love of Christ-following neighbors.
- For the Holy Spirit to empower us to love God and to love people.

SEEK GOD ON BEHALF OF
UNIVERSITY STUDENTS

Since my youth, O God, you have taught me, and to this day I declare your marvelous deeds.
— Psalm 71:17

Pray for many students to follow Christ; for the truth to radiate in a setting that is often hostile and cynical toward matters of faith; for students to make wise decisions, to form godly lifestyles and to shape their careers and ambitions to fulfill God's global purposes. Pray for leadership to be strong among Christian groups on campuses; for the advance of movements of prayer and mission mobilization; for the ministries that focus on students.

PRAYERWALK: *Pray for students at a place of higher education.*

SEEK GOD ON BEHALF OF
THE AMERICAS AND THE CARIBBEAN

Puerto Rico, Saint Kitts and Nevis, Saint Lucia, Saint Pierre and Miquelon

DAY 10

FRIDAY
FEBRUARY 27

Seek God...
to restore our families

SEEK GOD ON BEHALF OF
WOMEN

This woman was abounding with deeds of kindness and charity which she continually did.
— Acts 9:36 (NASB)

That women will be honored in their unique, God-created glory; that every kind of injustice toward women will cease; for pornography to be stopped; for protection from sexual violence; that hope would be renewed for the beauty of marriage and children; that single women would lay hold of God's full purpose in their lives.

PRAYERWALK: *Pray prayers of blessing for some of the women you come in contact with today.*

SEEK GOD ON BEHALF OF
THE AMERICAS AND THE CARIBBEAN

Saint Vincent and the Grenadines, Suriname, Trinidad and Tobago, Turks and Caicos Islands

---

He will turn the hearts of the fathers to their children, and the hearts of the children to their fathers; or else I will come and strike the land with a curse.
— Malachi 4:6

Turn our hearts to our elders in order that we might receive the heritage and life lessons they can impart to us. Renew our hearts for the coming generation, that we would aspire to see them walk in the fullness of Your blessing. Since our father Abraham's day we have known Your heart's desire to make Your people to become a blessing to all the peoples of earth. Hold back from striking the land with a curse. Instead, make Your people, parents and children together, to be a blessing to our city.

He said to her, "Go, call your husband and come here." ...They went out of the city, and were coming to Him.
— John 4:16, 30 (NASB)

In our city are many desolate women like this one, divorced more than once, separated from loved ones and without hope. You told her to summon the men who had once been married to her. And when they came, what did You say to them? You must have spoken words of life since they welcomed You as the Savior of the world. We pray that You would bring together the shattered pieces of many families in our city. Confront them with Your healing grace. Bring Your saving life to whole families. *Pray:*

- For God to heal the wounded hearts of parents and children who are alienated from each other.
- For Jesus to reveal Himself as the Wonderful Counselor, bringing peace in many homes.

Seek God...
to manifest His presence and glory

DAY 11

SATURDAY
FEBRUARY 28

My dwelling place will be with them;
I will be their God, and they will be My people.
Then the nations will know
that I the LORD make Israel holy,
when My sanctuary is among them forever.
— Ezekiel 37:27-28

Dwell among us as the most Holy God. Form us into the people that You have long desired. We will gladly fear You as much as we love You. We welcome You to preside over us, not merely to reside somewhere near us. Manifest the splendor of Your presence so greatly that reports about You spread throughout our communities and to distant places. Mark us with Your holiness so that we become notorious for the beauty of Your character in us.

....

The Word became flesh, and dwelt among us,
and we saw His glory,
glory as of the only begotten from the Father,
full of grace and truth. — John 1:14 (NASB)

Jesus, in Your flesh You anchored heaven's life on earth. None of us imagines that we have known You in all Your fullness. But anyone who encounters You has glimpsed something of the glory of the living God. Open our eyes to see You clearly and to know You in Your fullness. Your words are not merely true, You are truth itself. You are not merely giving and forgiving, You are God's gift itself. Finish what You came for: to make Your dwelling amidst Your people. *Pray:*

- For Christ to fill our attention and master our affections.
- For God to reveal Himself as holy and magnificent to people throughout our community.

SEEK GOD ON BEHALF OF
GANGS

"Because of the devastation of the afflicted, because of the groaning of the needy, now I will arise," says the LORD. "I will set him in the safety for which he longs."
— Psalm 12:5 (NASB)

That God will satisfy their deep desires for significance and belonging; for God to break the spiritual and social powers that hold them; for caring Christians to embrace them in the authentic love of God's family; for blessing upon the neighborhoods they claim.

....

PRAYERWALK: *Pray at a place affected by gang activity. Speak God's Word as you walk to spiritually "tag" the territories with unseen but real declarations of Christ's lordship, love and blessing.*

SEEK GOD
ON BEHALF OF

THE AMERICAS AND THE CARIBBEAN

United States of America, Uruguay, Venezuela, Virgin Islands of the USA

PAGE 15

WEEK 2 MARCH 1 - MARCH 7

PRAYING TOWARD HOPE

SPIRITUAL AWAKENING of LOST and BROKEN PEOPLE

This week we will pray for those who do not yet follow Christ, that God would wake them from spiritual slumber. We will pray that God moves in the lives of many people, to awaken them and draw them to Himself. We will seek God in hope that many will come alive to God at the same time. Past records of widespread spiritual awakenings show that such movements were always sought by God's people in persistent prayer.

ASIA AND THE PACIFIC

During the 40 days, we are praying for the continental areas of the earth in reverse sequence of Acts 1:8. This week we will pray for the peoples, cities, churches and families of Asia and the Pacific region.

Seek God...
to call people to sincere repentance

DAY 12

SUNDAY
MARCH 1

*Seek the LORD while He may be found.
Call on Him while He is near.
Let the wicked forsake his way
   and the evil man his thoughts.
Let him turn to the LORD,
   and He will have mercy on him,
   and to our God, for He will freely pardon.*
                             – Isaiah 55:6-8

You are always seeking us. But there are crucial moments when You suddenly draw people close to You. Bring such a day throughout our city. Free people from their self-defending thoughts which bind them and blind them to their evil ways. You know the ones who at this very moment are ready to open their lives to You. Soon they will choose to either follow You or to forget You. Draw near to them as they begin to draw near to You. Persuade their doubting hearts of Your magnificent love.

* * *

*For this people's heart has become calloused.
   They hardly hear with their ears,
   and they have closed their eyes.
Otherwise they might see with their eyes,
   hear with their ears, understand with their hearts
   and turn, and I would heal them.*   – Matthew 13:15

Many have heard the gospel before, but have rejected You. We call on Your mercy to give them another chance! Don't allow them to stumble on, hardened in heart, deaf to Your voice and blinded to Your glory. Open their eyes to Your beauty and open their ears to Your wisdom. Open their hearts to sense Your passionate love. If there is the slightest bit of turning toward You, consider it enough to grant them a day of healing and repentance. *Pray:*

- For God's kindness to confront and heal people who are hardened to the gospel.

- For opened eyes, softened hearts and receptive minds so that people hear the gospel and trust Christ.

SEEK GOD ON BEHALF OF
GOVERNMENT LEADERS

I urge, then, first of all, that requests, prayers, intercession and thanksgiving be made for everyone — for kings and all those in authority.
           – 1 Timothy 2:1-2

That they will be examples of righteousness to our society; that they will experience God's wisdom in their deliberations; that they will speak and carry out dealings with truth; that they will not hinder the service and worship of Jesus Christ; that they will come to know, honor and follow Christ.

PRAYERWALK: *Visit a center of city, county, state or federal government. Pray on or near the site. Leave a short note for a particular official which describes your prayers for God to bless him or her.*

SEEK GOD
ON BEHALF OF
ASIA AND THE PACIFIC

Afghanistan, American Samoa, Antarctica, Australia, Bangladesh, Bhutan, Brunei, Cambodia

PAGE 17

DAY 13

MONDAY
MARCH 2

Seek God...
to draw the lost with persistent love

SEEK GOD ON BEHALF OF
DEPRESSED PEOPLE

But God, who comforts the depressed, comforted us...
— 2 Corinthians 7:6

That God's healing presence will reach them; that the light of truth will dispel lies and the oppressive power of Satan; for helpful counsel; for the healing of long-standing wounds of mind and soul; that they would know the comfort and joy of the Holy Spirit; for the renewing of their minds in Christ.

PRAYERWALK: *Pray for people you see today who may be downcast, even though they appear to be cheerful and strong.*

SEEK GOD ON BEHALF OF
ASIA AND THE PACIFIC

China-People's Republic, China-Taiwan, Christmas Island, Cocos (Keeling) Islands, Cook Islands, Fiji

Yet the LORD longs to be gracious to you;
He rises to show you compassion.
For the LORD is a God of justice.
Blessed are all who wait for Him!...
How gracious He will be when you cry for help!
As soon as He hears, He will answer you.
— Isaiah 30:18-19

Be quick to answer when people cry to You for help. You are as swift as You are patient. We often think that You move much too slowly, but every act of Your mercy is a one-of-a-kind, perfectly timed stroke of kindness. You gaze upon each of us throughout every minute of our lives, vigilant for the times we cry out for help. Then You act with premeditated passion to bring us back to You. Wait no longer, God of patient love. May this be the day when You satisfy Your desire to be known as the God who is gracious to all.

So he got up and went to his father. But while he was still a long way off, his father saw him and was filled with compassion for him; he ran to his son, threw his arms around him and kissed him. — Luke 15:20

Father, You are constantly watching for Your long-lost sons and daughters to come home to You. Expose the hoax of worldly treasures that has deluded them. Awaken their yearning for You. Run toward them as they come. Convince them of Your unchanging love, regardless of what they have done or how long they have been away. Let the homecoming party begin. *Pray:*

- For Christians to express the Father's honoring love to those who are on their way back home to God.
- That God would strengthen the hearts of parents who wait for wayward children to come home.

Seek God...
to display His mercy

DAY 14
TUESDAY
MARCH 3

For as high as the heavens are above the earth,
  so great is His love for those who fear Him.
As far as the east is from the west,
  so far has He removed our transgressions from us.
As a father has compassion on his children,
  so the LORD has compassion on those who fear Him.
                          – Psalm 103:11-13

Why is Your boundless compassion unknown by so many who live in our city? Your love is more fiercely loyal than the finest father's love. Your constant compassion is more sure and merciful than the best of mothers. Display the uniqueness of Your love. Put Your kindness on exhibit. Send a message to people throughout our city that You long to embrace them with love as large as the sky.

· ·

But the tax collector stood at a distance. He would not even look up to heaven, but beat his breast and said, "God, have mercy on me, a sinner."
I tell you that this man, rather than the other, went home justified before God.   *– Luke 18:13-14*

We are qualified to stand before God as sinners with the people of our land. So we can sincerely cry, "Have mercy on us, a sinful people!" Every day we live in the consequences of piled-up sins of many generations. We see no easy way out. But since there is a mountain of love beneath every act of Your mercy, we refuse to despair. Instead, we are desperate in hope of Your love. Move in great mercy upon us all, O just and loving God. *Pray:*

- For Christians to pray with humility on behalf of people in their city.
- For people to experience God's justice in light of His great love in Christ.

SEEK GOD ON BEHALF OF
FATHERS

Fathers, do not exasperate your children; instead, bring them up in the training and instruction of the Lord.
                – Ephesians 6:4

That fathers will look to God as the ultimate spiritual head of their household, serving and caring for their families; that God will instill a vision for wholesome, supportive fatherhood among the fathers of the city; that absentee fathers would change their lifestyles to nurture their wives and children; that children will see the character of the heavenly Father in the lives of their dads.

· ·

PRAYERWALK: *Pray for the fathers in your workplace or near your home.*

SEEK GOD
ON BEHALF OF
ASIA AND THE PACIFIC

French Polynesia, Guam, Hong Kong, India, Indonesia, Japan, Kiribati

DAY 15

WEDNESDAY
MARCH 4

Seek God...
to satisfy spiritual hunger

SEEK GOD ON BEHALF OF
ELDERLY PEOPLE

They will still bear fruit in old age, they will stay fresh and green, proclaiming, "The LORD is upright; He is my Rock." — Psalm 92:14-15

That God's strength and peace will be poured out on everyone who is advanced in years. Pray that they may be honored, that they may be cared for; that loneliness be banished through lasting friendships and family bonds; that sickness be lifted; that they may live to see their prayers answered; that their latter years will be significant, reflecting the glory of God.

PRAYERWALK: *Pray for the oldest person you know in your neighborhood. Or pray at a retirement community or an extended care facility.*

SEEK GOD ON BEHALF OF
ASIA AND THE PACIFIC

Korea-North, Korea-South, Laos, Macau, Malaysia, Maldives, Marshall Islands, Micronesia

Some wandered in desert wastelands...They were hungry and thirsty, and their lives ebbed away. Then they cried out to the LORD in their trouble, and He delivered them from their distress... Let them give thanks to the LORD for His unfailing love and His wonderful deeds for men, for He satisfies the thirsty and fills the hungry with good things.
— Psalm 107:4-6, 8-9

So many people have never tasted, or even dared to imagine, the feast of life in You, Lord Jesus. They may not be aware that they are hungry and thirsty to know You. They may never have cried out to You for help. So we come to You on their behalf. Open the way for them to experience the abundant life of Christ. Surprise them and satisfy them with good things. Fill them with eternal life that begins right now.

When he came to his senses, he said, "How many of my father's hired men have food to spare, and here I am starving to death! I will set out and go back to my father..."
— Luke 15:17-18

In Your mercy, allow circumstances to reveal the emptiness of self-sufficient lives. May those far from You become nauseous with their sin. Cause them to recall something good about You and turn their attention toward You. And when they turn toward You, meet them at that moment. Reveal Your great love. Summon them home with hope that You will restore their lives to something better than they have ever imagined. *Pray:*

- For people to recognize the emptiness of life apart from the goodness of God's house.
- For prodigals to come home.

Seek God...
to overcome spiritual death

DAY 16

THURSDAY
MARCH 5

*Some became fools through their rebellious ways
  and suffered affliction because of their iniquities.
They loathed all food and drew near the gates of death.
Then they cried to the LORD in their trouble,
  and He saved them from their distress.
He sent forth His word and healed them;
He rescued them from the grave.* — Psalm 107:17-20

Today we pray for so many who are dying in spirit, body and soul. We, like they, have foolishly pursued distorted desires. We understand how minds become addled and bodies are addicted. We know how disappointment can hold hearts hostage in despair, so that people expect nothing new or true. And so we pray with understanding for those who are locked in spiritual prisons that they themselves have made. Send Your life-giving word and raise them to life again by the power of Your risen Son. Draw them from living death. Heal them to walk in Your life.

* * *

I tell you the truth, a time is coming and has now come when the dead will hear the voice of the Son of God and those who hear will live. — John 5:25

Risen Jesus, You said that the time has already come for the dead to hear Your voice. Call forth those who are entombed in spiritual graves. Do not let them escape the power of Your call. Speak so that even deaf ears hear Your life-giving summons. Those who hear will live! *Pray:*

- For many to hear the voice of Jesus and awaken from spiritual sleep to follow Him.
- For Christ to empower His people to communicate the gospel with life-giving authority.

SEEK GOD ON BEHALF OF
AGRICULTURAL WORKERS

For the LORD your God will bless you in all your harvest and in all the work of your hands, and your joy will be complete.
— Deuteronomy 16:15

That God will abundantly bless families who farm, ranch or support agricultural industries; that they would follow Christ and find ways to be part of life-giving churches. Pray especially for migrant workers who sometimes face injustice and great difficulties.

PRAYERWALK: *Pray in a rural area for God's blessing on the land and the families that He has placed there.*

SEEK GOD ON BEHALF OF
ASIA AND THE PACIFIC

Mongolia, Myanmar, Nauru, Nepal, New Caledonia, New Zealand, Niue, Norfolk Island

DAY 17

FRIDAY
MARCH 6

Seek God...
to bring victory over evil powers

SEEK GOD ON BEHALF OF
HEALTH CARE WORKERS

Blessed is he who has regard for the weak; the LORD delivers him in times of trouble. The LORD will protect him and preserve his life; He will bless him in the land.
— Psalm 41:1-2

That God will equip health care workers of every kind to serve others with loving hearts; that God will bless them with perseverance and joy; that the pressure of their professions will not crush their families and friendships; that many will follow Christ.

PRAYERWALK: *Pray on or near the grounds of a hospital or clinic.*

SEEK GOD ON BEHALF OF
ASIA AND THE PACIFIC

Northern Mariana Islands, Pakistan, Palau, Papua New Guinea, Philippines, Samoa, Singapore, Solomon Islands

---

The LORD will stretch forth Your strong scepter from Zion, saying, "Rule in the midst of Your enemies." Your people will volunteer freely in the day of Your power. In holy array, from the womb of the dawn, Your youth are to You as the dew.
— Psalm 110:2-3 (NASB)

Mighty Messiah, You died to break the dominion of evil and You ascended to liberate its captives. You alone are crowned with power over every enemy. Now extend the scepter of Your authority over our communities. Break the grip of demonic powers that hold people in their sin. Cause these prisoners of spiritual war to hear Your word and rise to follow You. Release them to be a generation of newly redeemed worshipers, radiant in fresh holiness like dew in the light of dawn.

"Lord, even the demons submit to us in Your name." He replied, "I saw Satan fall like lightning from heaven. I have given you authority to trample on snakes and scorpions and to overcome all the power of the enemy. ...However, do not rejoice that the spirits submit to you, but rejoice that your names are written in heaven."
— Luke 10:17-20

Jesus, be our Captain! We are more thrilled about Your rise to glory than we are distracted by the downfall of Satan. Restrain us from waging vigilante warfare in our own strength. As You authorize us, we will act in Your authority, secure in Your covering which shields us from the enemy. Be our Champion! Rise to break the grip of dark powers that hold captive the ones You came to save. *Pray:*

- For people who are afflicted by demonic powers to be liberated by the power of the gospel.
- For Christ to be glorified by subduing evil powers that may be at work in the community.

Seek God...
to be praised by those who were lost

DAY 18

SATURDAY
MARCH 7

*In that day you will say: "I will praise You, O LORD.
Although You were angry with me, Your anger
    has turned away and You have comforted me.
Surely God is my salvation; I will trust and not be afraid.
    The LORD, the LORD, is my strength and my song.
    He has become my salvation."
With joy you will draw water from the wells of salvation.*
— Isaiah 12:1-3

We pray on behalf of those who fear Your anger and doubt Your love. And so they hide from You instead of seeking You. They are thirsty to know You, but afraid of what they do not know. Bring the gospel message to them! You have turned away Your anger by the cross of Christ. Draw them to the springs of life and bring the day of their salvation. Become to them as refreshing as a drink of cool water; as reassuring as a love song. As their fears turn to joy, strengthen them to sing openly in grateful praise.

• •

*Jesus said, "Go home to your family
    and tell them how much the Lord has done for you,
    and how He has had mercy on you."* — Mark 5:19

Let the good news of Your life-changing power ripple throughout the families and friendships of our city. Cause those who are newly transformed by the gospel to go public with their faith. Embolden those who have loved You for years so that they tell their story yet again. We have every reason to expect that You will do great things. But in the midst of Your miracles may Your mercy be what amazes us. Make Your love become spectacular. For Yours is the kingdom, the power and the glory. *Pray:*

- For fresh stories of God's work to be told and retold.
- That new believers will become extravagant worshipers.

SEEK GOD ON BEHALF OF
THE POOR

I know that the LORD secures justice for the poor and upholds the cause of the needy. — Psalm 140:12

For God to establish the poor so that their spiritual and physical needs are met with dignity and stability; that God will release them from cycles of oppression and despair; that God will reverse every curse and multiply blessing.

• •

PRAYERWALK: *Walk places of poverty and neglect. Ask the Holy Spirit to give you His eyes and His heart in order to pray from hope, not pity. What grieves or gladdens God as He walks amidst the poor?*

SEEK GOD ON BEHALF OF
ASIA AND THE PACIFIC

Sri Lanka, Thailand, Tibet, Timor Leste, Tonga, Tuvalu, Vanuatu, Vietnam, Wallis and Futuna

WEEK 3 MARCH 8 – MARCH 14

PRAYING TOWARD HOPE

GOD'S TRANSFORMATION of our COMMUNITIES

God intends to bring forth a display of His kingdom in every people and place. Whenever Jesus is served as Lord, people change. By His power they begin to love and to live like Him. At times, Christ rapidly brings newness of life to many people, all at the same time. In such seasons, society can be changed so greatly that we have come to call it transformation. This week we will pray for God to bring about significant transformation in many cities of the earth.

AFRICA

This week we will be praying for the cities, peoples, tribes and countries of the continent of Africa.

Seek God...
for devastated cities to be restored

DAY 19

SUNDAY
MARCH 8

*The Spirit of the Lord God is upon me...the LORD has anointed me to bring good news to the afflicted... So they will be called oaks of righteousness,
    the planting of the LORD, that He may be glorified.
Then they will rebuild the ancient ruins.
They will raise up the former devastations;
    and they will repair the ruined cities,
    the desolations of many generations.*
— Isaiah 61:1, 3-4 (NASB)

Place Your Spirit upon us in the same way You put Your Spirit on Your Son. Send us now to our own city and place us among the poor with words and deeds of freedom. Empower Your people to speak good news with such life that people are transformed. Do not let the changes fade as a passing fashion. Implant these newcomers in their own neighborhoods as permanent displays of Your life, as if they were growing together as a mighty tree. Give them Your Spirit so that they are charged with hope to bring renewal to desolate families and places. Be glorified in the very settings where You are now forgotten.

* * *

I must preach the kingdom of God to the other cities also, for I was sent for this purpose. — Luke 4:43

You are still fulfilling the same purpose in our day. You are pressing forward to peoples and places that have yet to see the demonstration of Your kingdom with power. Do not overlook a single town or village, ghetto or barrio, neighborhood or network. Cause the love of Your kingdom to be displayed and declared everywhere. *Pray:*

- For the gospel of Christ to be proclaimed so that God is glorified by newly changed lives in every part of the city.
- For believers to demonstrate the power and life of God's kingdom as Jesus did.

SEEK GOD ON BEHALF OF
CHILDREN

Let the little children come to Me, and do not hinder them, for the kingdom of God belongs to such as these.
— Mark 10:14

That children will hear the gospel and encounter Christ early in life; that God's great fatherly heart will be revealed with healing power to kids who have been wounded or disappointed by their parents; for lasting family stability; for excellence in education; for wisdom to be formed in their early days; for safety from violence and perversion; for laughter and joy.

PRAYERWALK: *Pray for kids in your neighborhood or pray near a school in any part of town. Pray for the entire family that surrounds some of the children that you see.*

SEEK GOD ON BEHALF OF
AFRICA

Angola, Benin, Botswana, Burkina Faso, Burundi, Cameroon, Cape Verde Islands

DAY 20

MONDAY
MARCH 9

Seek God...
to turn injustice to generosity

SEEK GOD ON BEHALF OF
MINISTRIES

Finally, brothers, pray for us that the word of the Lord will spread rapidly and be glorified, just as it did also with you. – 2 Thessalonians 3:1

That Christian ministries will be founded on God's truth, anointed by God's power and funded by God's people; for refreshed encouragement upon those who labor in specialized service designed to increase the impact of local churches.

PRAYERWALK: *Find a high point from which you can see much of the community. Pray that God would send needed Christian workers to your city and at the same time send Christian workers from your city.*

SEEK GOD ON BEHALF OF
AFRICA

Central African Republic, Chad, Comoros, Congo-Democratic Republic (Zaire), Cote d'Ivoire, Djibouti

---

*Because of the iniquity of his unjust gain
   I was angry and struck him.
I hid My face and was angry,
   and he went on turning away, in the way of his heart.
I have seen his ways, but I will heal him.
I will lead him and restore comfort to him
   and to his mourners.* – Isaiah 57:17-18 (NASB)

We are blessed with abundance. But instead of living in grateful generosity, our hearts have been seduced by the mirage of material things. We have consumed more than we need so that our appetite for things and experiences has become distorted. You have seen us for who we are. Expose our self-destructive ways. Please heal our wounded, wandering hearts. Re-calibrate our desires so that we rejoice in what You have given. Lead us in Your ways of blessing.

---

*All the people...began to mutter,
"He has gone to be the guest of a 'sinner'."
But Zacchaeus stood up and said to the Lord,
"Look, Lord! Here and now I give half of my possessions
   to the poor, and if I have cheated anybody out of
   anything, I will pay back four times the amount."
Jesus said to him,
"Today salvation has come to this house."* – Luke 19:7-9

You rocked the whole city when You brought salvation to Zacchaeus. People stood amazed in the streets the next day, holding bags of gold in their hands that Zacchaeus had returned to them. Bring salvation to our city in the same way. Visit the homes of the rich, the poor, the powerful, and even the criminal, so that many are changed and the entire city knows that it was Your doing. *Pray:*

- For God to turn the hearts of Christians from the intoxicating power of materialism.
- That wealth in our city would be used justly and given freely for good works.

Seek God...
to honor and lift those who are poor

DAY 21

TUESDAY
MARCH 10

Who is like the LORD our God,
   the One who sits enthroned on high,
   who stoops down to look on the heavens and the earth?
He raises the poor from the dust
   and lifts the needy from the ash heap;
He seats them with...the princes of their people.
He settles the barren woman in her home
   as a happy mother of children.   — Psalm 113:5-9

We praise You, Great King and Judge of all the earth, for the way You watch and act on behalf of those who are poor. We gladly welcome You to fix Your gaze upon our community. Examine the affairs of commerce. Consider our courts and ways of governing. We call on You to move swiftly to help those who are unjustly impoverished. By Your awesome goodness, lift, exalt and honor them with fresh dignity and hope. Give those who are wealthy the honor of extending Your hand of blessing to many others. May our city rejoice to see how just and kind You are to all people.

* * *

When He saw the crowds, He had compassion on them,
   because they were harassed and helpless,
   like sheep without a shepherd.   — Matthew 9:36

Great Shepherd, extend Your compassion to those of our city who feel helpless in difficult circumstances. Rescue people from the ruins of unjust poverty. You see them as Your sheep. Cause them to know You as their Shepherd. Gather them into the safety and joy of Your care. Bless them so greatly that they become Your servants, showing Your compassion to others. *Pray:*

- For Christ to help His people see their cities through His eyes.
- For Christ to restore families and renew relationships in broken homes.

SEEK GOD ON BEHALF OF
THE NEWS MEDIA

These are the things you are to do: Speak the truth to each other, and render true and sound judgment.
— Zechariah 8:16

For people throughout the industries of broadcast and print media to come to know Jesus personally; that attitudes of cynicism will be changed; for those who love Christ to be strengthened in wisdom; for a growing emphasis in their work on that which carries virtue and conveys the values of Christ's kingdom throughout the city.

PRAYERWALK: *Visit a media center, a broadcast station or a publisher of print media. Pray for some who are associated with that particular enterprise.*

SEEK GOD
ON BEHALF OF
AFRICA
Equatorial Guinea, Eritrea, Ethiopia, Gabon, Gambia, Ghana, Guinea, Guinea-Bissau

PAGE 27

DAY 22

**WEDNESDAY
MARCH 11**

Seek God...
to establish what is true and right

SEEK GOD ON BEHALF OF
NATIVE PEOPLES

*I will set My justice
for a light of the peoples.*
— Isaiah 51:4 (NASB)

For native peoples who live in or near your city to be honored for who they are and for all God intends them to be; that God would heal the wounds to our nation that have resulted from broken treaties and mistreatment; that the tribes will be treated justly and find their destiny and highest dignity; that churches will flourish among them and that God's praise will resound in native languages.

PRAYERWALK: *As you prayerwalk, consider the native peoples who first dwelt in the area that has become your city. Pray for their descendants.*

SEEK GOD
ON BEHALF OF
AFRICA

Kenya, Lesotho, Liberia, Madagascar, Malawi, Mali, Mauritania, Mauritius

---

*Truth has stumbled in the streets, honesty cannot enter.
Truth is nowhere to be found,
   and whoever shuns evil becomes a prey.
The LORD looked and was displeased
   that there was no justice...
He was appalled that there was no one to intervene;
   so His own arm worked salvation for Him,
   and His own righteousness sustained Him.*
— Isaiah 59:14-16

Truth has become scarce in the open squares of our society. What is publicized or televised is so diluted with falsehood that we no longer expect to hear leaders speak with integrity. Those who stand for what is right in Your sight are sidelined or derided as intolerant fools. Do not leave us in this darkness. We have no one who will set things right. We call on You to intervene as only You can. Reach in, as if reaching with Your own right hand, to stabilize those who stand for Your righteousness. Expose what is false. Sustain what is true so that we can walk in Your justice.

Teacher, we know that You are truthful and teach the way of God in truth, and defer to no one; for You are not partial to any. — Matthew 22:16 (NASB)

Many have honored You as a good teacher of religious things. But You are far more than a guru or a life coach. You not only say true things, You teach God's ways in every area of life according to what is utterly true. You are truth itself. No wonder You cannot be swayed by what is popular or by who might be powerful. We welcome You to our city as Teacher. Train many to walk in God's ways so that our entire society honors what is true and what is right. *Pray:*

- For the reality of truth to be recognized in public affairs of government, education, commerce and art.
- For many to seek Christ as the true teacher, learning to obey Him in every part of their lives.

PAGE 28

Seek God...
to grant repentance from our violent ways

DAY 23

THURSDAY
MARCH **12**

Let men call on God earnestly that each may turn from his wicked way and from the violence which is in his hands. Who knows? God may turn and relent,
   and withdraw His burning anger
   so that we shall not perish. — Jonah 3:8-9 (NASB)

God of justice and love, You have every right to be angry. The violent ways of our world must grieve You greatly. Media screens are filled with vengeance sold as entertainment. We either ignore it or find ourselves enjoying it. And yet, when young people become killers, we are at a loss to explain why. We call on You to help us. Turn us from hatred, fear and anger. Break the escalating cycles of revenge with Your forgiveness. Turn our hostility into hospitality so that our community displays a heaven-like peace that only Christ can bring.

• •

And one of them struck the servant of the high priest,
   cutting off his right ear. But Jesus answered,
"No more of this!" And He touched the man's ear
   and healed him. — Luke 22:50-51

We easily understand Peter's defensive rage as he struck out at those who opposed You. We have sometimes brandished religious weapons to defend sectarian supremacy. This has only resulted in people becoming deaf to Your voice. Reach out and touch those offended by Your followers. Heal the harm we have done and restore them by the same mercy that You showed that night in the garden. Call us again to join You in Your suffering and to follow You in Your ways. *Pray:*

- For people who feel that they have been wounded by Christians to be restored by Jesus.
- For Christ to speak to us, as He did to Peter, forbidding us to defend His cause with violence.

SEEK GOD ON BEHALF OF
SINGLE PEOPLE

One who is unmarried is concerned about the things of the Lord, how he may please the Lord.
— 1 Corinthians 7:32 (NASB)

Pray that Christ will fill singles' hearts with His love; that they may taste the satisfaction which is found only in God; that friendships will bring ample fullness of relationship; for sexual purity and simplicity of lifestyle; and strong marriages for those who desire them. Pray for those single by divorce or death, that they would find healing and new hope for life ahead.

• •

PRAYERWALK: *Bless those people who are single. Consider their story. Pray for their future and hopes.*

SEEK GOD
ON BEHALF OF

AFRICA

Mayotte, Mozambique, Namibia, Niger, Nigeria, Republic of Congo, Réunion

PAGE 29

DAY 24

FRIDAY
MARCH 13

Seek God...
to bring forth justice and mercy

SEEK GOD ON BEHALF OF
EDUCATORS

But everyone who is fully trained will be like his teacher.
— Luke 6:40

That teachers and mentors will impart godly wisdom to help form character in their students; for needed tools and proper facilities; for those who home-school their children; for renewed zeal for truth and virtue; that they would have opportunity to know God in Christ; that believers would know how to pray for their students.

PRAYERWALK: *As you walk around a school, pray for teachers, administrators and other staff.*

Is not this the kind of fasting I have chosen:
  to loose the chains of injustice...
  to set the oppressed free and break every yoke?...
Then your light will break forth like the dawn,
  and your healing will quickly appear.
Then your righteousness will go before you,
  and the glory of the LORD will be your rear guard.
— Isaiah 58:6, 8

Much of our culture has been devised to keep us consuming more and more. The system is designed to make us more selfish every day. Give us courage to turn away from the tyranny of constantly satisfying our desires. Turn our attention instead to those who are trapped in cycles of injustice. Give us ways to free those—near to us, or far away—who suffer under oppression. Transform the economic structures of our land to reflect the heaven-like goodness of Your kingdom. Bring a new time of blessing upon Your people. Heal our land so that there is such abundance that there is more than enough for everyone. Bring it like a day slowly dawning. Spotlight Your blessing upon and through Your people, so that stories of Your glory are told.

You have neglected the weightier provisions of the law:
  justice and mercy and faithfulness.
But these are the things you should have done
  without neglecting the others. — Matthew 23:23 (NASB)

We can excel in performing perfunctory religious duties without Your help. But apart from Your Spirit we fail to do what pleases You most. Do a new work of Your Spirit in Your people. Give us the joy of pursuing justice. Teach us the song of serving in mercy. Train us to be faithful in Your purpose. *Pray:*

- For God's people to liberate the oppressed from spiritual bondage and economic poverty so that God is glorified.
- For Christians to envision a God-wrought justice and to faithfully serve in mercy.

SEEK GOD
ON BEHALF OF
AFRICA

Rwanda, Saint Helena, Sao Tome and Principe, Senegal, Seychelles, Sierra Leone, Somalia, South Africa

Seek God...
for the fruit of His righteousness

DAY 25

SATURDAY
MARCH 14

*Righteousness and peace have kissed each other.
Truth springs from the earth,
    and righteousness looks down from heaven.
Indeed, the LORD will give what is good,
    and our land will yield its produce.
Righteousness will go before Him,
    and will make His footsteps into a way.*
                    — Psalm 85:10-13 (NASB)

Walk before Your people, Risen Christ. Breathe the life of heaven into our homes and workplaces. Guide us to follow in Your footsteps, opening a way to bring life where there is death. Walk through our city, transforming barren places into bountiful gardens. Where there is evil, implant what is good. Cause Your people to bear the fruit of Your Spirit, bringing joy in living according to Your righteousness and peace in relationships.

*Therefore I say to you, the kingdom of God
    will be taken away from you,
    and be given to a people, producing the fruit of it.*
                    — Matthew 21:43 (NASB)

Lord Jesus, You intend to make Your coming kingdom to flourish now on earth with the beauty and substance of heaven's life. Fill our nation with the richness of Your righteous character. Cause our cities to abound with the fruit of Your kingdom. There will be a promised people, who will exhibit Your love and life in their community. We want to be that people. Empower us to bring forth tangible signs of Your righteousness, peace and joy. *Pray:*

- For the Spirit of God to empower ordinary believers to live in the righteousness of Christ.
- For people to see and experience the fruit of the Spirit in schools, workplaces and homes.

SEEK GOD ON BEHALF OF
THE **UNBORN**

For He will deliver...the afflicted who have no one to help. He will...save the needy from death. He will rescue them from oppression and violence, for precious is their blood in His sight.   — Psalm 72:12-14

That these precious children will be acknowledged and honored by all; for each one to find sheltering homes; that the awful waste of their lives would cease; that they would come to Christ at an early age; for the parents of unborn babies, that God will turn their hearts toward their children.

PRAYERWALK: *As you pray for your neighbors, pray that God will break the power of self-centered lifestyles that disregard children, and that He will forgive and heal those who have harmed their children in any way.*

SEEK GOD
ON BEHALF OF
AFRICA
South Sudan, Sudan, Swaziland, Tanzania, Togo, Uganda, Western Sahara, Zambia, Zimbabwe

WEEK 4 MARCH 15 - MARCH 21

PRAYING TOWARD HOPE
EVANGELIZATION of EVERY PEOPLE

This week we pray toward the hope of a thoroughly evangelized world. God's promises reveal His global purpose. He will draw people to Himself from every tribe and tongue in worshiping, obedient movements. On the earth today, there are still a few thousand groups which lack such dynamic, Christ-following movements. This week, our confidence that God will be followed in every people group will encourage us to pray in hope for the peoples that God has brought to our own communities.

EUROPE AND CENTRAL ASIA

This fourth week we will direct our prayers with and for the people, churches and countries of Europe and Central Asia.

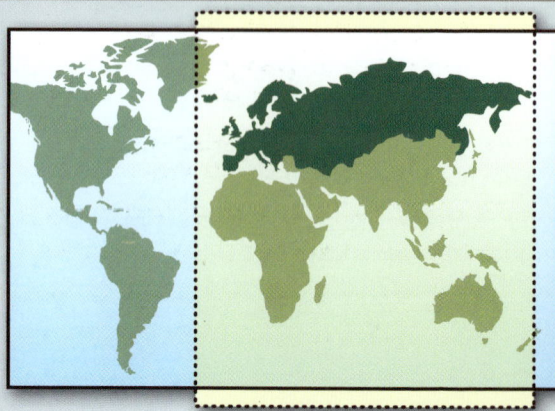

Seek God...
for His light to shine upon the nations

DAY 26

SUNDAY
MARCH 15

*It is too small a thing that You should be My servant
to raise up the tribes of Jacob...
I will also make You a light of the nations
so that My salvation may reach to the end of the earth.*
— Isaiah 49:6 (NASB)

Lift our vision to see the broad expanse of Your family. You are the Father of all peoples, always loving every people group, as if each of the nations was a precious child of Your household. Bring Your light to illumine every ethnic grouping, every racial sector, every language cluster, leaving no people beyond Your reach. Light of the world, make us to be Your light-bearers. We want our light to shine in faraway places. Yet send us as well to the nations who have been brought near to us in our city.

---

*For my eyes have seen Your salvation,
which You have prepared
in the presence of all peoples,
a light of revelation to the peoples,
and the glory of Your people Israel.*
— Luke 2:30-32 (author's translation)

Grant that we, too, may glimpse the fullness of the glory that You have prepared to display among the nations. The truth that brings God's salvation must be revealed. It can never be figured out by human understanding or recognized in nature. May the truth of the gospel shine like a great light among the diverse peoples of our city. Glorify Jesus as the only Savior, the light of the world. *Pray:*

- For Christians to recognize that God has prepared them to serve as light-bearers to the nations.
- That the light of the gospel would shine brightly among peoples who have not yet seen the glory of Christ as Savior.

SEEK GOD ON BEHALF OF
INTERNATIONAL VISITORS

Assemble the people — men, women and children, and the aliens living in your towns — so they can listen and learn to fear the LORD your God.
— Deuteronomy 31:12

For students, workers and businesspeople from other lands to be treated with honor and respect; that they will enjoy new friendships; that they will encounter the message of the gospel clearly declared and lovingly demonstrated.

PRAYERWALK: *Find a public place or business which draws international visitors or students. As you see people from different nations, pray God's blessing on them and their home countries.*

SEEK GOD ON BEHALF OF
EUROPE AND CENTRAL ASIA

Albania, Andorra, Armenia, Austria, Azerbaijan, Belarus, Belgium, Bosnia and Herzegovina, Bulgaria

DAY 27

MONDAY
MARCH 16

Seek God...
for His name to be honored among all peoples

SEEK GOD ON BEHALF OF
BROKEN FAMILIES

The LORD...sustains the fatherless and the widow.
– Psalm 146:9

Pray for healing of broken or embittered relationships; for comfort when a family member has passed away. Pray that the Father heart of God will overshadow children, that they would know the joy of being part of God's family; that God will meet financial needs, bring supportive friends and grant hope to many who come to follow Christ.

PRAYERWALK: *Apartment buildings often house fragmented families. Pray around an apartment complex, focusing prayers on those who have been bereaved or divorced.*

SEEK GOD ON BEHALF OF
EUROPE AND CENTRAL ASIA

Canary Islands, Croatia, Czech Republic, Denmark, Estonia, Faeroe Islands, Finland

---

My name will be great among the nations,
*   from the rising to the setting of the sun.*
In every place incense and pure offerings
*   will be brought to My name,*
*   because My name will be great among the nations.*
– Malachi 1:11

We know that You are praised on the other side of the planet. And yet people on the other side of our town have yet to see or know You. You are so worthy to be worshiped everywhere. But You can only be loved if You are known for who You truly are. Display Your magnificent power, so that You become famous in our city for Your singular greatness. But even more, demonstrate Your mercy so that many come to thank You for Your wondrous goodness. May the fame of Your name be great so that our entire community speaks of You with reverence and awe.

Our Father in heaven, hallowed be Your name.
– Matthew 6:9

Cause Your name to be sanctified, so that You are seen as utterly other than any man-made god. We want people throughout our city to recognize how unique and precious You are. May the story of what You have done in our lives confirm Your reputation throughout our community. May Your name become known with such widespread clarity that You will be worshiped, adored, loved and followed among all the peoples of the earth. *Pray:*

- That believers would become jealous for God's glory—that He would be known and honored.

- For false stereotypes and misconceptions about God to be exposed and the truth to be revealed.

Seek God...
for God to be revealed by hearing prayer

DAY 28

TUESDAY
MARCH 17

O You who hear prayer,
*   to You all people will come...*
You answer us with awesome deeds of righteousness,
*   O God our Savior, the hope of all the ends of the earth*
*   and of the farthest seas.* — Psalm 65:2,5

People have always prayed and You have always heard them. You always respond to the people who pray with great love and wisdom. Today we ask You to answer those who pray in conspicuous ways so that You become their hope. Listen to the cries of desperate people as they call out for help. Hear us as we pray on behalf of neighbors and friends. As You hear and respond to these prayers, do more than just what people request. Surprise many by helping them in ways that they did not ask. In the sight of those who pray, become more than a helper or a provider. Become for them a Savior, and so You will become the hope of all the earth.

* * *

The whole crowd of disciples
*   began joyfully to praise God in loud voices*
*   for all the miracles they had seen.* — Luke 19:37

Lord Jesus, each of Your miracles in the Bible was in some way an answer to prayer. In our day, outdo Yourself by answering prayer in miraculous ways. Enable us to pray for our friends with empathy and faith. Reveal Yourself by hearing the prayers of people far from You. Show Your kindness and power so that we can celebrate as Your disciples did, with the same loud, raucous joy. *Pray:*

- For God to encourage those who doubt with tangible signs of His goodness through answered prayer.
- That answered prayers would become the talk of the town.
- For those who pray to become those who know and trust God in a personal way.

SEEK GOD ON BEHALF OF
MEN

Let not the wise man boast of his wisdom or the strong man boast of his strength or the rich man boast of his riches, but let him who boasts boast about this: that he understands and knows Me.
— Jeremiah 9:23-24

That men will seek God and honor Him in faithfulness, wisdom and truth; for their identity to be centered in Christ-like servant leadership; that the vision of their lives would be to serve and advance God's purposes.

PRAYERWALK: *Ask God to help you focus prayers of blessing on one or two of the men that you see today.*

SEEK GOD
ON BEHALF OF

EUROPE AND CENTRAL ASIA

France, Georgia, Germany, Gibraltar, Greece, Hungary, Iceland, Ireland

DAY 29

**WEDNESDAY
MARCH 18**

Seek God...
for leaders to hear and know the truth

SEEK GOD ON BEHALF OF
PHYSICALLY DISABLED PEOPLE

In all their affliction He was afflicted...In His love and in His mercy He redeemed them; and He lifted them and carried them all the days of old.
— Isaiah 63:9 (NASB)

That they will be surrounded with loving friends and family; for steady refreshment of their hearts toward God; for physical stamina and healing; for financial provision to cover the cost of therapy and special care; that they will know and display the love of God.

PRAYERWALK: *Pray along the same route that a person with disabilities might use to move through your neighborhood, school or workplace. As you do, pray for someone you know with disabilities.*

SEEK GOD ON BEHALF OF
EUROPE AND CENTRAL ASIA

Italy, Kazakhstan, Kosovo, Kyrgyzstan, Latvia, Liechtenstein, Lithuania, Luxembourg

---

*May all the kings of the earth praise You, O LORD,
when they hear the words of Your mouth.
May they sing of the ways of the LORD,
for the glory of the LORD is great.*
— Psalm 138:4-5

Reveal Your glory to the kings, rulers and governors of the earth. Disclose the truth of Your supremacy in and over all things. Grant opportunities for the leaders of our land to hear Your word clearly, as if spoken directly from Your mouth. Instruct them in Your ways of wisdom. Move them to honor You with public praise and to allow Your people to sing in celebration of Your coming kingdom.

*"You are a king, then!" said Pilate.
Jesus answered, "You are right in saying I am a king.
In fact, for this reason I was born,
and for this I came into the world,
to testify to the truth.
Everyone on the side of truth listens to Me."*
— John 18:37

Jesus, You are the King of all kings. Rulers throughout history have recognized You, but many have defied Your rule. When You stood before Pilate, You fulfilled the purpose for which You came: to proclaim the truth, so that ultimately, many would be drawn into Your kingdom. Take Your stand again. Declare truth to the rulers of the world. Let them hear Your voice, listen to Your instruction and lead in accordance with Your word. *Pray:*

- For the uniqueness of Jesus to be revealed to those in positions of power.
- That the truth and beauty of Christ's kingdom would be recognized in the courts and councils of our cities.

Seek God...
for the gospel to be declared to all peoples

DAY 30

THURSDAY
MARCH 19

Sing to the LORD, praise His name.
Proclaim His salvation day after day.
Declare His glory among the nations,
  His marvelous deeds among all peoples.
For great is the LORD and most worthy of praise.
He is to be feared above all gods.   — Psalm 96:2-4

May the greatness of Your glory be declared openly throughout the earth! We are accustomed to Your praises, but in our day, how many people have not yet heard? How many clans, tribes or languages have yet to hear the full story of what You have done in Christ? You are worthy to be exalted with music, art and worship from every culture. Continue sending emissaries to distant lands as well as to the diverse peoples of our own city. Make us Your messengers to the peoples You have placed among us. We want to hear the global song of Your glory in our city.

When they saw Him, they worshiped Him...
Jesus came to them and said,
"All authority in heaven and on earth has been given to Me.
Therefore go and make disciples of all nations...
And surely I am with you always,
  to the very end of the age."   — Matthew 28:17-20

You promised to be with us every day until the end of the age. And so we know that You are present with us now, wielding the authority that the Father has given You. You are now drawing people from every language and culture to live under Your lordship. Leave no people unreached. Finish Your sending and empowering work. We bow before You in surrendered worship, willing to be sent and asking for Your kingdom to come. *Pray:*

- For local believers to work strategically to fulfill Christ's commission in their cities.
- For every people group represented in our city and community to hear the gospel.

SEEK GOD ON BEHALF OF
PRISONERS AND THEIR FAMILIES

You who seek God, let your heart revive. For the LORD hears the needy, and does not despise His who are prisoners.
— Psalm 69:32-33 (NASB)

That people in jails and prisons will hear the gospel and follow Christ; for fellowships of believers to multiply; that they be protected from violence and forces of spiritual evil; that the spouses and children of prisoners would be sustained, protected, provided for and honored rightly; that released prisoners find strength and wisdom to live abundant lives.

PRAYERWALK: *Pray near a jail or correctional facility. Or pray for homes in your neighborhood that may have family members or loved ones in prison.*

SEEK GOD ON BEHALF OF
EUROPE AND CENTRAL ASIA

Macedonia, Malta, Moldova, Monaco, Montenegro, Netherlands, Norway, Poland, Portugal

DAY 31

FRIDAY
MARCH 20

Seek God...
for entire cities to seek the living God

SEEK GOD ON BEHALF OF
MOTHERS

She is clothed with strength and dignity; she can laugh at the days to come. She speaks with wisdom… Her children arise and call her blessed; her husband also, and he praises her…
— Proverbs 31:25-26, 28

That God will powerfully refresh mothers in the honor and glory of motherhood; that they will be strengthened with grace, wisdom and love in serving their children; that they will be loved, protected and served by committed husbands; that mothers will model and express God's own nurturing love.

PRAYERWALK: *Walk through your neighborhood, praying for grandmothers and mothers.*

SEEK GOD ON BEHALF OF
EUROPE AND CENTRAL ASIA

Romania, Russia, San Marino, Serbia, Slovakia, Slovenia, Spain, Sweden

---

Peoples will come, even the inhabitants of many cities. The inhabitants of one will go to another, saying, "Let us go at once to entreat the favor of the LORD, and to seek the LORD of hosts; I will also go." So many peoples and mighty nations will come to seek the LORD of hosts.
— Zechariah 8:20-22 (NASB)

One person might be bold enough to say, "I am going!" in his eagerness to seek You. But only You can trigger chain reactions of people to move toward You with lasting passion and increasing momentum. Draw more than a few scattered individuals. Fulfill Your promise in our day by igniting city-wide movements. Cause one city-wide movement to energize another, so that many peoples throughout our city and the world will seek You.

The whole city was stirred and asked, "Who is this?" — Matthew 21:10

Jesus, as You entered the city on Palm Sunday, normal patterns of life were disrupted. You set an entire city buzzing with questions and conversations about You. You were the focus of everyone's attention. Once again, stir the hearts of many in our city to know the truth of who You really are. May their questions be answered by those who know You. Manifest Your presence to those who welcome You. *Pray:*

- That the city would be stirred with curiosity about Jesus.
- For Christians to speak openly and clearly about who Jesus is and how to follow Him.
- For skeptical or doubting friends to seek God.

PAGE 38

Seek God...
for worship from every nation

DAY 32

SATURDAY
MARCH 21

*All the ends of the earth
    will remember and turn to the LORD.
And all the families of the nations
    will bow down before Him,
    for dominion belongs to the LORD
    and He rules over the nations.* — Psalm 22:27-28

How long until You fulfill Your promise to be known in every nation? When will the global extravaganza of worship rise to You from all the peoples? Even now You are served with full-hearted worship, expressed in many different languages and cultures. But You are worthy of praise from every people and place. Draw some from every people. Gather those who love You in every city. Give them courage to honor You openly. Quickly bring the day when Your family is fully represented among all the families of the earth!

----

*Now there were some Greeks among those
    who were going up to worship at the feast.
These then came to Philip...and began to ask him,
    saying, "Sir, we wish to see Jesus."*
        — John 12:20-21 (NASB)

People from the nations are eagerly seeking to worship the true and living God. Regardless of how sincere they may be in their search, You are not to be found in religious rituals. The truth and life that they seek can only be found in Jesus. May many seekers be introduced to Jesus by Your followers. May those who seek to worship You become those who see and follow You. *Pray:*

- That those who are sincerely seeking to worship God will encounter Christ and become part of God's family.
- For believers from many churches to gather in city-wide worship events.
- For Jesus to be worshiped by people from every tribe and language.

SEEK GOD ON BEHALF OF
SUBSTANCE ABUSERS

On the day the LORD gives you relief from suffering and turmoil and cruel bondage.
— Isaiah 14:3

That God will break every form of bondage, including alcoholism and drug addiction. Pray for wise counselors to bring intervention and help. Pray that God will heal the minds and bodies of substance abusers; that they will turn from self-centeredness to living their lives for Christ.

PRAYERWALK: *Consider those in your neighborhood who may be bound by addiction to drugs or alcohol. Ask God to free them.*

SEEK GOD ON BEHALF OF

EUROPE AND CENTRAL ASIA

Switzerland, Tajikistan, Turkmenistan, Ukraine, United Kingdom, Uzbekistan, Vatican City

WEEK 5   MARCH 22 - MARCH 28

PRAYING TOWARD HOPE
RECONCILIATION
among the PEOPLES

During this final week we will be praying that God will bring substantial healing to relationships among the peoples of the world. We will pray that God moves swiftly to heal the racism and prejudice that we experience in our own cities, as well as in the conflicts that simmer in places devastated by oppression and strife.

THE MIDDLE EAST

During this fifth week, our prayers will be focused on the peoples and countries of the Middle East.

Seek God...
to bring forth peace among peoples

DAY 33

SUNDAY
MARCH 22

*He will judge between many peoples
 and will settle disputes for strong nations far and wide.
They will beat their swords into plowshares
 and their spears into pruning hooks.
Nation will not take up sword against nation,
 nor will they train for war any more.* — Micah 4:3

We are powerless to quell the rivalries and feuds that rage among the nations. Jealousies seem to be settled, but rise up again. Even small incidents can provoke new rounds of violence. So we come before You, God of all the nations. You have promised to preside as judge and to resolve every dispute. Only when You rise to rule will the nations find rest from war. We do not know when or how You will do this. But Your promise gives us courage to ask You to begin this work of peace even today. Disarm our hearts and dismantle grievances between racial and social groupings. Walk with us and train us in Your ways of peace.

* * *

*But the tax collector stood at a distance. He would not even look up to heaven, but beat his breast and said, "God, have mercy on me, a sinner."
I tell you that this man, rather than the other, went home justified before God.* — Matthew 12:21

Glorify the name of Christ throughout all peoples, cultures and nations. As they hear what changes Jesus has brought to entire communities, stretch their expectations for what their people could become. Release the hopes and dreams which You have hidden in the heart of every nation. Fix their hope entirely on Jesus as He fulfills their longings for peace. *Pray:*

- For the Prince of Peace to overcome tensions between ethnicities in our city.
- That Christ would be revealed as the greatest hope for sustained peace between cultures and peoples.

SEEK GOD ON BEHALF OF
ETHNIC COMMUNITIES

All the ends of the earth will remember and turn to the LORD, and all the families of the nations will bow down before Him. — Psalm 22:27

That God will bring racial harmony; that long-standing offenses may be healed by the forgiveness that begins in Jesus; that Christians show honor and act in Christ's reconciling power; that the beauty of distinctive languages and cultures would be on display in local churches.

PRAYERWALK: *Pray blessings in a neighborhood with an ethnic identity different than your own; or pray blessings upon a business owned by people of another ethnicity than yours.*

SEEK GOD
ON BEHALF OF
THE MIDDLE EAST
Algeria, Bahrain, Cyprus

DAY 34

MONDAY
MARCH 23

Seek God...
to be exalted in troubled times

SEEK GOD ON BEHALF OF

JUDGES AND LAW ENFORCEMENT

Blessed are they who maintain justice, who constantly do what is right. — Psalm 106:3

Pray for wisdom, principled patience and gentle authority; for physical and emotional protection; for strength and blessing for their families; that they will become agents of God's hand to resist evil and bring an environment in which heaven's justice can increase.

PRAYERWALK: *Pray outside the nearest police station or court. Leave a short personal note for judges or police leaders letting them know how Christians are praying for them today.*

SEEK GOD ON BEHALF OF

THE MIDDLE EAST

Egypt, Iran, Iraq

I will shake all nations,
  and the desired of all nations will come,
  and I will fill this house with glory...
The glory of this present house
  will be greater than the glory of the former house...
And in this place I will grant peace. — Haggai 2:7, 9

Come Lord Jesus. You are the desire of all nations. Build Your house amidst the chaos of this age. Nations are shaking. Once-solid institutions are shifting. Evil runs unchecked. You promised that in just such a day of global dread a great Desired One would arise. Shake people loose from the lesser things that entangle them. Awaken desire for the greater glory of Christ. Gather a great throng of people to Yourself. Under the canopy of Your presence, let heaven's peace be granted and Jesus be exalted.

Nation will rise against nation, and kingdom against kingdom. There will be famines and earthquakes in various places. All these are the beginning of birth pains... And this gospel of the kingdom will be preached in the whole world as a testimony to all nations, and then the end will come. — Matthew 24:7-8, 14

Bitter conflicts are tearing peoples and countries apart. Natural disasters have obliterated entire coastlines and cities, filling our hearts with fear. But Your kingdom is forever. It must be proclaimed. Enable us to be the living testimony of Your kingdom. Display evidence of the excellence of Your reign. Demonstrate how You reconcile races and heal the wounds of war. *Pray:*

- For the gospel of the kingdom to be communicated powerfully in the midst of conflict and uncertainty.
- For churches to publicly testify to Christ's kingdom with faith and boldness.
- For people to follow Christ without fear in the midst of difficult days.

Seek God...
for Christ's followers to seek and make peace

DAY 35

TUESDAY
MARCH 24

*Seek the peace and prosperity of the city
to which I have carried you into exile.
Pray to the LORD for it, because if it prospers,
you too will prosper.* — Jeremiah 29:7

Forgive us for speaking of our city with ridicule and pessimism. We have failed to believe Your intentions to bring peace and blessing here. You love this community and desire to bring good upon all. So we pray, expecting to become part of the answer: Bring Your peace and prosper the people of this city. Let them know that You are blessing them. Bring outbreaks of peace so that everyone in the city can celebrate together.

---

*But I tell you who hear Me: Love your enemies.
Do good to those who hate you.
Bless those who curse you.
Pray for those who mistreat you.* — Luke 6:27-28

We want to believe that we have followed Your ways of love. But often we are merely nice without being kind; pleasant without being sincere toward people who are not like us. We know that we are commanded to love our enemies, but we struggle to do so. There may be those who dislike or oppose us because of You. Nevertheless, change our hearts, shape our thoughts and direct our deeds so that we become the blessing You desire us to be. *Pray:*

- That Christians would respond to opposition by doing good in Jesus' name.
- For persecuted believers around the world to experience God's strength and encouragement.

SEEK GOD ON BEHALF OF
HOMELESS PEOPLE

But He lifted the needy out of their affliction and increased their families like flocks.
— Psalm 107:41

Pray for immediate relief, shelter, food and health care; that Christ will restore hope for the future; for wise counsel and trustworthy friendship; for protection from the risks of life on the streets; for employment, housing and restored family life.

PRAYERWALK: *Visit a place where homeless people seek shelter or employment. Pray God's blessing on the people you see who appear to be homeless.*

SEEK GOD ON BEHALF OF
THE MIDDLE EAST
Israel, Jordan, Kuwait

DAY 36

WEDNESDAY
MARCH 25

SEEK GOD ON BEHALF OF
THE ATHLETIC INDUSTRY

Yours, O LORD, is the greatness and the power and the glory... Wealth and honor come from You...In Your hands are strength and power to exalt and give strength to all.
— 1 Chronicles 29:11-12

Pray for those in support roles and those with higher profiles, that they will know Christ and fulfill God's calling in their lives. Pray that athletes would be good examples of dedication, commitment and courage; that they will live with integrity and carry out the responsibility of wealth and reputation; that God will reveal His calling and purpose for students and coaches in high school and university programs.

PRAYERWALK: *Pray on-site at the scene of an upcoming sports event near you.*

SEEK GOD ON BEHALF OF
THE MIDDLE EAST

Lebanon, Libya, Morocco

Seek God...
to be honored even in the midst of war

Come and see the works of the LORD,
　　the desolations He has brought on the earth.
He makes wars cease to the ends of the earth.
He breaks the bow and shatters the spear...
"Be still, and know that I am God;
I will be exalted among the nations,
　　I will be exalted in the earth."　　— Psalm 46:8-10

You are the only one who can bring warfare to a standstill. Bring an end to the raging wars that burn in many parts of the earth. Declare reconciliation among the racial feuds that smolder in our cities. Disarm and justly crush tyrants who seek to rule by terror. We plead for a peace so great that Your promised blessing will come to all peoples. Be exalted in the midst of the nations, Almighty God. Be honored for the power of Your love. Be exalted in all the earth.

Everyone who falls on that stone
　　will be broken to pieces,
but he on whom it falls will be crushed.
— Luke 20:18

You constantly show mercy to all, even to those who have launched wars against You and have mistreated those called by Your name. We pray for these who have made themselves Your enemies. Give them opportunity to be broken and remade. Grant them grace to fall upon You so that they are not ruined and shamed by the coming of Your mighty lordship. You are as merciful as You are mighty. Even Your enemies will praise You. *Pray:*

- That brokenness and humility would characterize Christians in our city.
- For Christ to be honored by the reconciliation of longstanding conflicts in our city.

DAY 37

Seek God...
for Christ to gather the nations in worship

THURSDAY
MARCH 26

*Let this be written for a future generation,
that a people not yet created may praise the LORD...
So the name of the LORD will be declared...
when the peoples and the kingdoms assemble
to worship the LORD.* — Psalm 102:18, 21-22

Your written promise must come forth: You will gather and form a great worshiping people from all peoples of the earth. This new people will name You with praise that will be loud and long, a great crescendo at the end of the age. Cause Your global people formed in Christ to praise You openly with overtones of that final song. May churches long divided by doctrines and traditions become united in public worship that exalts the name of Christ. May the open assembly of Your people in worship across the face of the earth become a spectacle of Your reconciling power.

"Is it not written: 'My house will be called a house of prayer for all nations'?" — Mark 11:17

You said that You would build a house "made without hands." You are still building this house of prayer with worshipers from all the nations. Be pleased to draw to Yourself many diverse styles of song and celebration from every people. May other nations no longer be held back from presenting to You gifts from the redeemed glory of their cultures. Gather us in our cities as beautiful, multifaceted expressions of Your house of prayer. *Pray:*

- That God would be offered creative new expressions of worship from different ethnicities of the city.

- That the world would see different churches united in worship and service for Christ's glory.

SEEK GOD ON BEHALF OF
LABORERS

How blessed is everyone who fears the LORD, who walks in His ways. When you shall eat of the fruit of your hands, you will be happy and it will be well with you.
— Psalm 128:1-2 (NASB)

Pray that God will reveal the dignity and honor of doing work as unto Christ; that workplaces would be a setting of safety, joy and friendship; for workers to be treated with justice and dignity; for continued employment in the changing global economy; for many to follow Christ and serve Him openly in the workplace with co-laborers.

PRAYERWALK: *Almost every community has factories, construction sites or other places of industry. Pray for the laborers in these places.*

SEEK GOD
ON BEHALF OF

THE MIDDLE EAST
Oman, Qatar, Saudi Arabia

DAY 38

FRIDAY
MARCH 27

Seek God...
to instruct the peoples in His ways

SEEK GOD ON BEHALF OF
REFUGEES

He defends the cause of the fatherless and the widow, and loves the alien, giving him food and clothing. And you are to love those who are aliens, for you yourselves were aliens in Egypt.
— Deuteronomy 10:18-19

For safe, legal immigration and for conditions to improve in homelands so that extended families will be united; for Christians to open homes and hearts to them; for the gospel to be conveyed clearly; for those desiring to return to homelands to be granted asylum and repatriation; that God would open the way for those desiring a new home to be resettled.

PRAYERWALK: *Pray prayers of welcome, protection and blessing for refugees and immigrants in your community.*

SEEK GOD ON BEHALF OF
THE MIDDLE EAST
Syria, Tunisia, Turkey

In the last days the mountain of the LORD's temple will be established...and all nations will stream to it. Many peoples will come and say,
  "Come, let us go up to the mountain of the LORD,
  to the house of the God of Jacob.
  He will teach us His ways,
  so that we may walk in His paths." — Isaiah 2:2-3

In the last days You promised to summon the nations to learn Your ways. Despite the high ideals of our nation, we have not mastered basic righteousness or kindness. We have failed to flourish in peace. We must be taught and guided if we are ever to walk in Your ways. Even today, train the peoples of our land to live in justice, joy and generous love. Teach our children. Instruct our elders. Train our leaders. Educate our educators. Lead us to walk in the wisdom of Your ways.

At dawn He appeared again in the temple courts,
  where all the people gathered around Him,
  and He sat down to teach them. — John 8:2

Your words were so appealing and powerful that people rose at dawn and crowded near to hear You. We have not been as eager to hear Your teaching. Forgive our complacency. Thrill us with the hope that we will live in a city changed by Your teaching. Gather us to Yourself. Disciple us in the hope of heaven filling earth. *Pray:*

- That anointed teaching of God's Word in our city would draw many to Him.
- That seekers would bring their questions and concerns to Jesus.
- That a new dawn would arise in our city as many people gather around Jesus.

Seek God...
for the nations to welcome Christ's lordship

DAY 39

SATURDAY
MARCH 28

Rejoice greatly, O Daughter of Zion!
...See, your king comes to you, righteous
and having salvation, gentle and riding on a donkey,
on a colt, the foal of a donkey...
He will proclaim peace to the nations.
— Zechariah 9:9-10

Your kingdom does not come like a military conquest. Instead of invasion, You come by invitation. And so we gladly welcome Your visitation. Come gently, but victoriously. Come, lifting Your voice to proclaim Your peace to the nations and to our city. Disarm the arguments of those who deny You. Dismantle the defenses of those who resist Your love. Give us hope for enduring days of peace that only You can bring.

"Look how the whole world has gone after Him!"
— John 12:19

The people on that first Palm Sunday welcomed You. They had come for the usual religious ceremonies. Instead, they found the city exploding, joyously welcoming someone as the long-awaited Messiah. We want the people of our city to recognize the day of Your visitation. Disclose Yourself to them, Lord Jesus! Make Yourself known to all who have dared to desire that You will do great things in these days. *Pray:*

- That God's Spirit would open people's hearts to welcome the beauty and life-changing power of Christ's lordship.
- That God would bring a day of dynamic movements in which many people follow Christ together.

SEEK GOD ON BEHALF OF
BUSINESS PEOPLE

But remember the LORD your God, for it is He who gives you the ability to produce wealth.
— Deuteronomy 8:18

Ask God to bless those who base business practices in righteousness. Pray that God will prosper those who pursue their business as mission for God's kingdom. Pray for the gospel to spread in the marketplace; for righteous managers and executives; for creative, godly entrepreneurs. Pray that God would frustrate plans which escalate injustice.

PRAYERWALK: *As you pass through a place of business today, pray for Christ to be followed and for His name to be honored in that setting. Pray for God to bless the endeavors that exemplify His kingdom.*

SEEK GOD ON BEHALF OF
THE MIDDLE EAST
United Arab Emirates, Yemen

> The event we have come to call "Palm Sunday" shines as a prophetic portrait of the spiritual awakening that Christ desires to bring.

Seek His VISITATION
Welcoming Christ our King

The crowds... were shouting, "Hosanna!... Blessed is He who comes in the name of the LORD!" ...All the city was stirred, saying, "Who is this?"
– Matthew 21:9-10

The event we have come to call "Palm Sunday" shines as a prophetic portrait of the spiritual awakening Christ desires to bring. Jesus not only initiated the procession, but He refused to shut it down. He was doing more than merely fulfilling prophecy. He was prophesying, presenting a lasting vision of how He will be recognized in the midst of hostility at the end of the age. Christ will be followed by some in every people. He will be welcomed, at least by a few, in every place. Palm Sunday gives us a vision of the global spiritual awakening we are praying toward.

Preparing the way by prayer

Jesus prepared the way for Palm Sunday by sending His followers to pray on-site in many communities (Luke 10:1-2). The prayers of these ordinary followers were publicly prayed and then openly answered. God was being honored. Jesus was becoming famous in places where He had not yet personally visited. The expectancy of what God would do was great.

A crescendo of welcoming praise

The raising of Lazarus touched off an explosion of welcoming praise (John 12:18). The dramatic answer to Jesus' prayer for His friend Lazarus (John 11:41-43) got everyone talking about all they had seen God do in the lives of their friends and neighbors. Luke says the crowd was praising God "for all the miracles which they had seen" (Luke 19:37). Grateful praise for many answered prayers quickly became a crescendo of welcoming worship.

> Whenever there has been revival, it has been a partial fulfillment of the promise of Palm Sunday.

Palm Sunday: The Hope of Christ's Visitation

A lasting movement

Thousands of people gathered at the temple with Jesus early every morning, hanging on His every word (Luke 21:38). The Palm Sunday worshipers should not be confused with the much smaller mob which shouted for Jesus' execution later in the week. That crowd was incited by Christ's enemies, who were forced to arrest Jesus by night "because they were afraid of the people" —the very throng that had welcomed and honored Him daily with increasing devotion (Luke 22:2, Mark 14:1-2).

A prophetic portrait

Palm Sunday is sometimes dismissed as if it were a political rally gone wrong. But Jesus was for it. He planned whatever could have been planned. And He refused to silence the celebration. He said that rocks would have cried out if the people had been restrained (Luke 19:40). The intensity mounted. The crowds increased. Eventually "all the city was stirred, saying, 'Who is this?'" (Matthew 21:10). Those who hadn't yet personally encountered Jesus were eager to know more. If Jesus was giving us any indication of how God desires to visit communities with transforming power, we are right in praying for such receptive glory to sweep throughout whole cities.

The hope of visitation: His arrival more than our revival

Hated or praised, Christ was then what He will be again: the sole focus of attention of whole cities in days of great spiritual awakening. Our best prayers are prayers of welcome—that the risen Jesus Himself will be recognized and received throughout entire communities. Whenever there has been revival, it has been a partial fulfillment of the promise of Palm Sunday. Now, more than ever, it's time to invite Christ the Lord to bring His life-giving presence upon our cities.

WEEK 6 MARCH 29

Seeking GOD
...for Christ to VISIT our communities with His presence and saving power

The earth is the LORD'S, and all it contains, the world, and those who dwell in it...
  He shall receive a blessing from the LORD
    and righteousness from the God of his salvation.
This is the generation of those who seek Him,
    who seek Your face — even as Jacob.
  Lift up your heads, O gates, and be lifted up, O ancient doors,
    that the King of glory may come in!
Who is the King of glory? The LORD strong and mighty, the LORD mighty in battle.
  Lift up your heads, O gates, and lift them up, O ancient doors,
    that the King of glory may come in!
Who is this King of glory? The LORD of hosts, He is the King of glory.
— Psalm 24:1, 5-10 (NASB)

We approach You with the boldness of Jacob, who refused to stop wrestling with You until You blessed him. You were not offended by his tenacity. Like Jacob, we have yet to see Your promises fulfilled. So we boldly approach You, day after day, seeking Your blessing on our families and our cities.

Beyond tangible blessing, our hearts desire Your presence and Your glory. Our greatest request: Open the gates of heaven! Come through and enter the earth which You have made. Invade the cities which we have made.

The fullness of the earth is Yours, but it is empty without Your glory. So again, we cry: Open the gates of heaven and come! With Your blessing, bring Your glory.

And when You come, we will know You. We will know You because of the many days we have sought You. We know who You are: You are the King of glory! Subdue Your enemies. Who can withstand You? You are the only rightful King. You are power itself. You are the Lord Almighty. Open the ancient doors. Come fill the earth with Your glory!

Seek God...
for Christ to be welcomed as King

DAY 40

SUNDAY
MARCH 29

"Blessed is the King who comes in the name of the Lord!
   Peace in heaven and glory in the highest!"
Some of the Pharisees in the crowd said to Jesus,
   "Teacher, rebuke Your disciples!"
"I tell you," He replied, "if they keep quiet,
   the stones will cry out." — Luke 19:38-40

As we celebrate Your coming to Jerusalem on Palm Sunday, we release our hearts to leap forward in hope that You will visit our city–and every city–to bring a great awakening to Your lordship. How can people be silent if You are present in their midst, demonstrating the splendor of Your kingly rule? May the rocks keep silent before the growing sound of welcoming worship! May our children be the first to know and honor You. May millions submit their lives to You and be saved. Let Your peace be as great as Your glory.

He who testifies to these things says,
   "Surely I am coming quickly." Amen.
   Even so, come, Lord Jesus!. — Revelation 22:20 (NKJV)

We yearn for Your coming. Yet our best statement of hope is to say "Even so..." The way and time of Your coming is Yours to choose. Whatever You might mean by "quickly," we trust Your love and wisdom. No matter how long we might wait, find our hope fixed on You. Only come, and come to us quickly. *Pray:*

- That our city would awaken to Christ's lordship.
- That believers would remain resolute in their hope for Christ's return at the end of the age.

SEEK GOD ON BEHALF OF
THE COMING GENERATION

How often I have longed to gather your children together, as a hen gathers her chicks under her wings...you will not see Me again until you say, "Blessed is He who comes in the name of the Lord."
— Matthew 23:37, 39

That many who are now small children would soon become passionate followers of Christ; that during their lifetimes they will finish evangelizing the world; that they will endure suffering to overcome evil and bring forth the promised blessing of God upon all peoples; that they will give Christ the finest whole-life worship of all history.

PRAYERWALK: *Walk your city thinking of the people who will live there in years to come, should the Lord tarry. Pray for the generation that will be dwelling in your city when Jesus returns.*

SEEK GOD ON BEHALF OF
JERUSALEM

Pray for God's peace and glory to be upon Jerusalem

Co-working with God in the story of His love
God's persistent kindness

When did God begin to do good things in your life? Was it only after you became a Christian?

Actually, the Bible is very clear about God doing good things in people's lives long before they even know about Him. There's a story of kindness in every person's life. God delights in showing His premeditated, forever love with tangible acts of kindness. Here's why: The Bible says that "the kindness of God leads you to repentance" (Romans 2:4).

God's kindness never coerces us. Instead, His goodness "leads" us through the events of our lives to the point where we can turn, or repent. God will never force people to turn around. We have to do our own turning.

Follow God's great desire. God is motivated with unstoppable passion to regain relationship with people. He deeply "desires" that "all people" would "come to the knowledge of the truth" about Him (1 Timothy 2:4). Knowing the truth about God can open a relationship with Him. That's what being "saved" is all about.

Co-work with God. Because of His constant desire for every single person to know Him, God gives us two simple but powerful ways to work with Him:

1. **Pray for every person.** God wants us to pray for every person. "First of all, I urge that...prayers, petitions and thanksgiving be made on behalf of all people" (1 Timothy 2:1).

2. **Convey and display the message with perfect timing.** God gives us opportunity to make clear the message about Jesus with divine timing, "the testimony [to be] given in its proper time" (1 Timothy 2:6).

Our part isn't hard.
Caring prayers, tangible kindness and well-timed words

Why pray at all? There's joy in it. God doesn't need our prayers to act. He doesn't really need our efforts to serve people. But He does want us to experience the joy of co-working with Him (and with others who are praying with us!) in bringing new life to others. As you keep attentive to what God may be doing, don't be surprised if God opens opportunities for you to express His love in tangible ways.

Pray along with what God is already doing. Since God's work is always a story, your best praying will be part of an ongoing story. Instead of using prayer as a quick-fix procedure that supposedly gets results if performed correctly, your prayer is a way of collaborating with God.

God is already on the move. Prayer does not push God to get started. He's already doing good things in everyone's life. And He desires to do even better things. Instead of holding off the worst, think of your prayers as asking God to bring on the best.

Persistent, life-giving **prayer** for others leads to opportunities to **care,** displaying God's love, which opens the way to **share** the gospel, declaring God's love.

A simple sequence: Prayer-Care-Share.
On the following pages, we (Steve Sjogren and Steve Hawthorne) offer some proven ideas for how you can pray for others. As you pay attention and take notice of what God may be doing in their lives, you'll often find that there are simple ways for you to do small acts of kindness that can reveal God's great love. Putting God's love on display often opens ways to present the gospel with sensitivity and clarity.

Life-giving prayer

Pray your way into their story
by Steve Sjogren with Steve Hawthorne

There's a story rolling in everyone's life. God has done and will do good things in people's lives. He does good things long before anyone opens their life to Christ.

It's the kindness of God that leads anyone to repentance (Romans 2:4). Meeting, following and serving Christ is always a lifelong story. The typical stories have multiple encounters and experiences that turn people closer to or further from Christ. Someone researching effective ways to lead people to Christ found that most people have no less than five significant encounters in which the message of the gospel registers at the heart level.

As we connect with people in practical ways, those deep heart connections increase rapidly. I love to assume that God is on the verge of doing something good in the lives of everyone I see in order to bring about yet one more significant encounter with His love. I enjoy getting in on the story by praying my way, or "noticing" my way into what God may be up to next.

Praying for people is the simplest way I know to start seeing them from God's point of view—to notice what they're facing or to get a hunch about what God may have underway.

Prayer *leads to* **care,**

Prayerwalk
to get in step with what God is doing

When we live at too fast a pace, we can miss God's invitations to become part of the story He's unfolding in people's lives. Prayerwalking is a way to slow down and begin to naturally pick up on the concerns of God. His heart begins to merge with ours. We allow what causes Him excitement or anguish to affect us in the same way.

Prayerwalking is praying near the people you are praying for, in the places where they live or work. Prayerwalking isn't really about walking around. It's praying with your eyes and heart wide open so you can take notice of what God may be wanting to do in their lives. You can pray quietly with your eyes open without people necessarily knowing that you are praying for them. Be on the scene without making one.

What to pray
You don't have to have an official "prayer request" to start praying creatively. Try praying in these three ways:

1. **Thank your way into God's story.** How has God provided, protected or guided them? We're told to offer "thanksgiving on behalf of all people" (1 Timothy 2:1). When you think about it, it's not hard to do. What you're doing is "noticing" what God may be doing. Such "noticing" makes it easier to pray and easier to see what part God may give you in what's coming next.

2. **Notice what they may be facing.** What fears, pain or ambitions are driving them? What relationships or disappointments have paralyzed them? What turmoil or crisis may be overwhelming them? Pray accordingly.

3. **Pray with scripture.** Check out the passages of scripture in the side margins of the pages throughout this booklet. Many of them can give you ideas about what you can pray.

opening ways to **share** the gospel.

Practical ways to care

From noticing to nudging
A small kindness can show great love

As you pray for others, "noticing" what God is doing in their lives, you allow God to point out needs as well as opportunities. It's as if He is "noticing" through you.

Often, those needs work as your cue that it's your time to play a bit part in the story. In the flow of what is unfolding in people's lives, God uses small acts of kindness to reveal the great love of Christ.

Kindness is never accidental. It's always intentional. Get creative. Team up with others. Dream up ways to serve people in small, tangible ways. You might call it committing acts of non-random kindness.

Many fear sharing the gospel because they think that they'll have to be pushy. No one likes pushy people. So don't be pushy. Instead of pushing, your act of kindness may "nudge" them closer to the time when they will open their life to Christ. Those around me are gaining courage as they see how uncomplicated it all is. Just show God's love in small ways and see where it goes.

> **Great resources for many more good ideas**
> Steve Sjogren has developed some good resources designed to help ordinary people show God's love in practical ways. He's got hundreds of tested ideas. Go to **www.KindnessResources.com**.
>
> *"I highly recommend Steve's resources. He makes it fun."* — Steve Hawthorne

Prayer *leads to* **care**

Demonstrate
God's love in a practical way

Nudging people with God's love can be done thousands of ways. It's God's love. You don't have to feel it. Just find some simple way to display the smallest kindness. I define it this way: Demonstrate the kindness of God by offering to do some act of humble service with no strings attached.

For people near you who know you

Show your concern naturally by doing "golden rule" kindness: Do something for others that you are already going to do for yourself. Almost any simple errand you can do at work or household chore can be extended to those you know. Some ideas:

- **Watch the kids.** Offer to watch your neighbor's kids so they can do some errands or just take a break.
- **Write a note.** Birthday, holiday, or figure out something to thank them for.
- **Move the cans.** Drag their garbage cans back off the street on trash day.
- **Buy extra flowers.** "Accidentally" on purpose buy too many flowers for your home and bring some to a neighbor.
- **Shovel the driveway.** Clear the snow for someone else before you do yours.
- **Bake too many.** Bake cookies. Make enough to share.
- **Go for coffee.** If you're going for coffee, ask if you can get some for a co-worker. Or just surprise them. A week later they may want to go along with you to talk.

For people you don't know — yet

Team up with others to display some kindness in a public setting to people you've never met. Do it with no strings attached and without any sermons. Just do helpful things. Always explain what you are doing by saying something like: "We're doing a free community service project to show God's love in a practical way." Conversations will get going easily. You'll have fun and be able to notice what God may be doing in their lives.

Distribute inexpensive but helpful stuff like cool drinks or popsicles when it's hot. Or provide a simple service that can be done quickly such as washing windows, raking leaves, cleaning toilets, clearing gutters, washing cars and hundreds more.

opening ways to **share** *the gospel.*

Engaging ways to share

Connecting the stories
Listening in order to tell

As you "notice" your way into the story of people's lives by sincerely serving them or praying for them, you'll become convinced that there are new chapters and better endings in their story than they may have ever dreamed.

How do you tell them about it? It's tempting to think that you have to tell or sell the gospel as a powerful, sermon-like speech. Instead of blasting away, do some "story-listening." That can turn into "story-exchanging," which leads to the best gospel story-telling.

Many avoid evangelism because it usually puts pressure on those who speak and those who listen. It gets clouded with fear and guilt on both sides.

I've been watching for the moments that God makes to convey even a little bit of the gospel. It takes the pressure off and puts it on God. Even small bits of banter with people can unfold into some amazing conversations. He really is present in their life story, even as we talk.

It's fun to point out what God may have already been doing in their lives, to explain how they can know Him better. And nudge them on their way.

Prayer *leads to* **care**

Relate the gospel story with their story

"Crossing over" may be easier than you think

I find that many hesitate to do what I call "crossing over" into other people's lives. It's really a matter of engaging in conversations. Usually the crossing over never happens because we are waiting for some kind of open door to spontaneously happen. That's just too much waiting. While we wait for God to open doors, we will often find that He's already unlocked them.

Try doing this: Make up an excuse to connect with people. Sometimes I borrow things from people even when I don't really need anything. At work I have borrowed paper or a pen or a stapler for an hour. Upon returning the item, it is natural to engage in a few minutes of conversation. With neighbors I've borrowed ingredients (for the cookies I bring over later), or tools that I may not urgently need. The key is to find a reason to "stop on by." It may be to borrow something, or it may be to give them something. You might never know your neighbors if you don't "stop on by."

Watch for three stories

God is bringing together His story with their story. Watch how three stories intersect and overlap:

- **Their story.** How do they tell their own story? Keep listening to what's important to them.

- **Your own "Jesus story."** By your own "Jesus story" I mean the saga of how God has been doing things in your life that brought you into relationship with Jesus. As you know, that story is still unfolding. You are still being changed by Christ.

- **The gospel story.** By the gospel story I mean what God has been doing in lives, cities and nations through the ages. It's a story, of course, that centers on what Christ has done, is doing and will do. There are hundreds of ways to tell God's story.

Find ways to get into conversations with others about their life and their story. Listen well and you'll find ways that your story corresponds to something of theirs. You'll find it natural to exchange parts of your story with theirs. You can explain how Jesus has come to play a major role in your life. From there it's not hard to tell the greater gospel story as you have come to know Christ and walk with Him.

opening ways to **share** the gospel.

PRAYERCONNECT

Connecting to the heart of Christ through prayer

A new bimonthly magazine designed to:

Equip prayer leaders and pastors with tools to disciple their congregations.

Connect intercessors with the growing worldwide prayer movement.

Mobilize believers to pray God's purposes for their church, city and the nations.

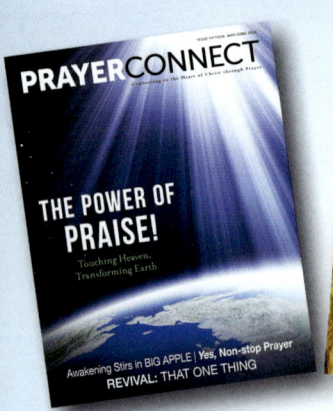

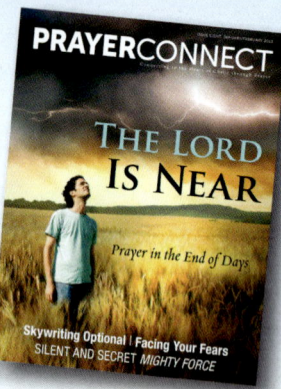

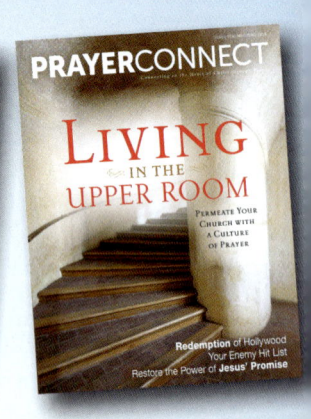

Each issue of **PRAYER**CONNECT includes 48 pages of:
- Practical articles to equip and inspire your prayer life.
- Helpful prayer tips and proven ideas.
- News of prayer movements around the world.
- Theme articles exploring important prayer topics.
- Connections to prayer resources available online.

Three different ways to subscribe *(six issues a year)*:

$24.99 - **Print** *(includes digital version)*

$19.99 - **Digital**

$30.00 - **Membership** in Church Prayer Leaders Network
(includes print, digital and CPLN benefits)

Subscribe now.
Order at www.prayerconnect.net or call 800-217-5200.

PRAYERCONNECT is sponsored by: America's National Prayer Committee, Denominational Prayer Leaders Network and The International Prayer Council.

FreshPrayer

Pray from ancient truths for urgent needs

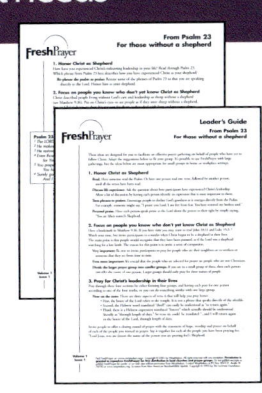

FreshPrayer is a free, single-page prayer guide, available on the WayMakers website (waymakers.org). Each issue is designed to help you find clear, relevant ways to pray from specific scriptures for particular needs and concerns of people who are far from Christ.

Scripture-rich authority. Life-giving clarity. Everyday simplicity.

It's perfect for small groups looking for innovative ways to pray together for people who don't yet know Christ.

Ideas for those who facilitate gatherings.

Every issue consists of two items: a single-page participant's guide to be copied for everyone in your group; and a single-page leader's guide that provides ideas to guide lively prayer sessions. The "pdf" files can be downloaded from the WayMakers website. It's an ideal way to continue to pray beyond *Seek God for the City*.

Guided, grounded and focused.

The most engaging prayer gatherings are usually **guided** by a facilitator who invites participants to form simple and sincere requests that are **grounded** in the truths of the Bible and **focused** on specific issues in the lives of others.

Each issue contains a leader's guide and a participant's guide. Download FreshPrayer at no cost at **waymakers.org**.

Put a copy in the hands of everyone who gathers to pray. Selected verses are laid out alongside creative ideas that help people unite and focus intercessory prayer for those without Christ.

Calling Christians to pray for the Muslim world

The 24th Annual
30 Days of Prayer for the Muslim World

June 18 to July 17, 2015

Join millions of Christians around the world who participate each year in this largest ongoing international prayer focus on the Muslim world.

Coinciding with Ramadan, Christians worldwide are called to make an intentional effort to learn about, pray for and reach out to Muslim neighbors—across the street and around the world.

Media sound bites about Islamic extremism can too easily incite anger, fear and even hatred toward Muslims. Instead, pray with the mind and heart of Christ. This full-color prayer guide —available in both adult and kids versions— is a proven tool helping Christians to understand and to persistently pray for Muslim neighbors and nations.

Calling Christians to pray with Faith, Hope and Love since 1993

To find out more, or to order booklets go to:
www.30DaysPrayer.com
email: paulf@30DaysPrayer.com

Or write:
WorldChristian.com "30 Days"
PO Box 9208
Colorado Springs, CO 80932

WORLDCHRISTIAN.COM
books, prayers and tours that impact lives

30 Days of Prayer
PRAYING FOR OUR WORLD

Pray with the world.

THE GLOBAL Day of Prayer

**Pentecost Sunday
May 24, 2015**

Focus prayer with the Ten-Day Prayer Guide, available in pdf format online. Unite the prayers of your congregation with churches across the globe on Pentecost Sunday using the "Prayer for the World."

- **One day of prayer on Pentecost Sunday, May 24, 2015**
- **Ten days of continuous prayer, May 14 - 23, 2015**
- **Ninety days of blessing, May 25 - August 22, 2015**

Since the dawn of this century, Christians all over the world have gathered on Pentecost Sunday for a day of repentance and prayer. Many gatherings have been large-scale public events. Even more have been small gatherings in churches and homes. Find all you need on the website: a downloadable Ten-Day Prayer Guide, resources to help congregations pray the "Prayer for the World" on Pentecost and an all-new guide for the ninety days of blessing.

For info and prayer guides go to
www.gdopusa.com or
www.globaldayofprayer.com

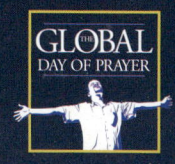

GLOBAL DAY OF PRAYER

WayMakers Resources

ITEM	DISCOUNT	COST *	QUANTITY	TOTAL
SEEK GOD FOR THE CITY 2015				
or CLAMA A DIOS POR LA CIUDAD 2015**				
1-19 copies		$ 3.00 each		
20-99 copies	20%	$ 2.40 each		
100-249 copies	35%	$ 1.95 each		
250-499 copies	55%	$ 1.35 each		
PROMPTS FOR PRAYERWALKERS		$ 2.00 each		
LIGHT FROM MY HOUSE		$ 2.00 each		
OPEN MY CITY		$ 2.00 each		
WHAT WOULD JESUS PRAY?		$ 2.00 each		
BLESSINGS		$ 2.00 each		
THE LORD IS THEIR SHEPHERD		$ 2.00 each		
PRAYERWALKING	25%	$ 9.00 each		

SHIPPING & HANDLING
- $ 1 – $ 10 $ 5.00
- $ 11 – $ 30 $ 7.00
- $ 31 – $ 75   20% of order
- $ 76 and up   13% of order

Subtotal
Texas residents add 8.25% sales tax
Shipping and Handling (Minimum $5)
Donation to WayMakers (Optional)
TOTAL

PLEASE SHIP TO: *(Please provide a street address. UPS cannot deliver to a Post Office Box.)*

Name

Organization

Street Address

City   State   ZIP

Phone   E-mail

VISA / MC / Discover   Expires

Name on card

* Please call to learn about quantity discounts (up to 60%) on most items!

** ***Seek God for the City*** in Spanish is available at the same prices. Order online, or call us to combine English and Spanish in the same order. ***Clama a Dios por la Ciudad*** está disponible al mismo precio que en inglés. Llámenos para combinar libros en inglés y español en la misma orden.

Please order early to allow normal delivery time of two weeks (but many orders can be fulfilled last-minute!). Order Seek God for the City before January 30 to be sure of getting all the copies you need. Additional shipping costs may be required after February 6.
Please include payment with your order. Please calculate and include payment for shipping costs. Thanks! For quick delivery, call us.
Make checks payable to WayMakers. Please send this form with payment to:

WayMakers
PO Box 203131
Austin, TX 78720-3131

Phone (512) 419-7729
       (800) 264-5214
Fax   (512) 323-9066
Web   www.waymakers.org